Fire On H[illegible]

An Anthology of Contemporary Women's Poetry

Kelli Russell Agodon & Annette Spaulding-Convy

Editors

Two Sylvias Press

Editors: Kelli Russell Agodon and Annette Spaulding-Convy

Cover Art Photo Credit: Nance Van Winckel, *UNITED ATARAXIA*

First Edition. Created in the United States of America.

ISBN-13: 978-0615961835

For information on purchasing and downloading *Fire On Her Tongue: An eBook of Contemporary Women's Poetry* and to learn more about Two Sylvias Press, please visit www.twosylviaspress.com

Editors' Note

The blood jet is poetry,
There is no stopping it.
~Sylvia Plath

Two Sylvias Press has received many inquiries about releasing *Fire On Her Tongue: An eBook Anthology of Contemporary Women's Poetry* in a print version, and to accommodate those requests, we have converted the format from eBook to print book. The print version of *Fire On Her Tongue* is not a second edition of the anthology: no poems have been revised, no bios have been updated. The only minor change is in the formatting of each poet's acknowledgments and bio pages, which have been combined and serve as an introduction to the poet's work.

Our goal in soliciting work for this anthology was to create a selection of poems that represents some of the best women poets writing today. Of course, this list of "best women poets writing today" is not complete. We had difficulty contacting some of the poets we most admire, a few choosing not to submit their work, several missing the deadline, and others who simply did not receive our emails or did not have current contact information available. If we could have our complete "wish list" of favorite poets in this anthology, it would have twice the number of pages. We believe the poems we have chosen reflect the dynamic themes of the contemporary woman's experience and are superbly crafted, but know that some of our favorite poets are missing.

Fire On Her Tongue proudly features over seventy women who are currently active in the poetry world. Their ages range from thirteen to ninety-one. They are urban and rural. They are academics, professionals, stay-at-home moms. They are the poets you have already read and admire, featured at poetry festivals across the world, and they are the poets you will read for the first time, about whom you will say, "How is it that I've never heard of her?" And you will add her to your list of favorites.

As poets ourselves, we are honored to assemble this group of incredible women and make available their work to a wider audience. As readers, we're thrilled to have *Fire On Her Tongue* to share with our friends and other poetry readers. And as women, we are empowered that we live in a world where an idea for a poetry collection can become a reality, give birth to an independent press, and be shared with you.

~ *Kelli Russell Agodon & Annette Spaulding-Convy*
Editors, Two Sylvias Press, 2011 / 2014

Table of Contents

If I read a book and it makes my whole body so cold
no fire can ever warm me, I know that is poetry.

~Emily Dickinson

Kim Addonizio

Kim Addonizio is a poet and novelist. Her latest books are *Lucifer at the Starlite*, recently a finalist for the Poets' Prize; and *Ordinary Genius: A Guide for the Poet Within*, both from W.W. Norton. Addonizio's honors include a Guggenheim and two NEA Fellowships. She has been awarded the Pushcart Prize in both poetry and the essay. Her collection *Tell Me* was a National Book Award Finalist. She offers workshops in Oakland, California where she lives, and online. www.kimaddonizio.com

Acknowledgments

"Them" and "What the Dead Fear" appear in *The Philosopher's Club* (BOA Editions, 1994)
"Let's Get Lost" appears in *Poet Lore*
"Please" appears in *New Letters*

Let's Get Lost

Let's get lost, in a romantic mist…
~ Chet Baker

I am insanely attracted to you.
Please make me an inmate in your asylum
and give me a bad prognosis.
These characteristics qualify me
to become your new girlfriend:
I am portable and flexible.
My eyelids click like a doll's.
My doll heart is teeming
with bioluminescent organisms.
Also, I have a keychain that meows.
Just press the button.
Let's get bathetic.
Let's get sloshed
in a glass of crushed ice
under a pygmy umbrella.
Let's go find the primitives
who collect vinyl records,
who still write letters and believe
we're gods when we stumble
into their village, thirsty and tired,
so they throw an all-night party
with lots of dancing and flames
and a stellar jazz ensemble.
Dear morning star,
are you my boyfriend yet?
I am still infectious.
Please come down with me.

Them

That summer they had cars, soft roofs crumpling
over the back seats. Soft, too, the delicate fuzz
on their upper lips and the napes of their necks,
their uneven breath, their tongues tasting
of toothpaste. We stole the liquor
glowing in our parents' cabinets, poured it
over the cool cubes of ice with their hollows
at each end, as though a thumb had pressed
into them. The boys rose, dripping, from long
blue pools, the water slick on their backs
and bellies, a sugary glaze; they sat easily on high
lifeguard chairs, eyes hidden by shades,
or came up behind us to grab the fat we hated
around our waists. For us it was the chaos
of makeup on a bureau, the clothes we tried on
and on, the bras they unhooked, pushed
up, and when they moved their hard
hidden cocks against us we were always
princesses, our legs locked. By then we knew
they would come, climb the tower, slay anything
to get to us. We knew we had what they wanted:
the breasts, the thighs, the damp hairs pressed flat
under our panties. All they asked was that we let them
take it. They would draw it out of us like
sticky taffy, thinner and thinner until it snapped
and they had it. And we would grow up
with that lack, until we learned how to
name it, how to look in their eyes and see nothing
we had not given them; and we could still
have it, we could reach right down into their
bodies and steal it back.

Please

I was cruel but you were cruel first,
cried the rose to its thorn
before sending it away,
then making dinner alone
and toppling into a wine glass,
falling into bed with petals askew.
Love is a bluebird from hell.
Love is a teacup Chihuahua.
I love you means my mouth is full
of darkling beetle grubs
and if I fall off your lap I may die.
I'm sorry love isn't a flower.
I'm sorry my heart is a sinkhole.
It swallowed a freezer once.
You were right to go. But come back.
Cried the rose. Coughing up
a few thawing pork chops.

What the Dead Fear

On winter nights, the dead
see their photographs slipped
from the windows of wallets,
their letters stuffed in a box
with the clothes for Goodwill.
No one remembers their jokes,
their nervous habits, their dread
of enclosed places.
In these nightmares, the dead feel
the soft nub of the eraser
lightening their bones. They wake up
in a panic, go for a glass of milk
and see the moon, the fresh snow,
the stripped trees.
Maybe they fix a turkey sandwich,
or watch the patterns on the TV.
It's all a dream anyway.
In a few months
they'll turn the clocks ahead,
and when they sleep they'll know the living
are grieving for them, unbearably lonely
and indifferent to beauty. On these nights
the dead feel better. They rise
in the morning, and when the cut
flowers are laid before their names
they smile like shy brides. Thank you,
thank you, they say. You shouldn't have,
they say, but very softly, so it sounds
like the wind, like nothing human.

Deborah Ager

Deborah Ager's poetry collection is *Midnight Voices*. She's received fellowships and scholarships from the MacDowell Colony, the Sewanee Writers' Conference, the Mid-Atlantic Arts Foundation, Virginia Center for the Creative Arts, and the Atlantic Center for the Arts and is founding editor of *32 Poems Magazine*. With John Poch and Bill Beverly, she's editing the *32 Poems Magazine Anthology* (forthcoming 2012). She's working with Matthew Silverman on a Jewish American Poetry anthology. www.deborahager.com

Acknowledgments

"Mangos" appears in *Delaware Poetry Review*
"Fires on Highway 192" appears in *Los Angeles Review* as "Fires"

Fires on Highway 192

after Neruda's "Disasters"

In Florida, it was raining ash because the fire
demanded it. I had to point my car landward
and hope the smoke would part, but it was a grey sea
absorbing my body. Cabbage palms were annihilated.
Even the Indian River steamed. Black stalks stank.
The condominiums spit smoke into twilight.
Still, a cattle egret landed, preening, in a pasture
filled with embers—the cattle dead or removed.
And I was hungry; there was nothing to eat.
And I was thirsty and raised the river to my mouth.
And I was alone, and there was only that one egret
searching for a cow. The wind was a whisper on my tongue.
Ash on ash. Slumber shallow. I was a frown
in an unfamiliar city after sundown. Vultures circled
like assassins. I made a bed of the road. I made a pillow
of misery and slept and had no story I wanted to confess.

Mangos
Tampa, 1942

If they liked mangos, we'd have none,
mama says. We move yard to yard.
We squat and bend to pick up fruit.
She slides her full hand deep into the sack
to keep the fruit from bruising. I see a curtain
move in the house and wish for better clothes.
My dress has holes—too small to see,
mama says. But even a needle does nothing
to fabric this thin. The threads I've sewn
hang over holes like a weak bridge.
The sun is a torch on my burnt ear tips;
it won't let up. I am dreaming of yellow
meat, sweet threads sewing my tongue quiet.
I know how to make one piece of toast last,
not to complain when my back throbs.
My hands slip over the smooth mango skin.
The air is an oven and won't let up—
not even for two hungry women
calculating how long this fruit will last.

Ivy Alvarez

Ivy Alvarez is the author of *Mortal* (Red Morning Press, 2006) and three chapbooks. A recipient of writing residencies from MacDowell Colony (USA), Hawthornden Castle (UK) and Fundación Valparaiso (Spain), her poems appear in journals and anthologies in many countries and online. Several of these have been translated into Russian, Spanish, Japanese, and Korean. Born in the Philippines and raised in Australia, she has lived in Wales, UK since 2004. Her second book of poems is imminent. www.ivyalvarez.com

Acknowledgments

"What Rita Hayworth Threw Away" appears in *Page Seventeen*, Issue 8 (Australia, 2010)
"What Vivien Leigh Dropped" appears in *OCHO #24* (USA, 2009)

What Vivien Leigh Dropped

Larry's Hamlet; I mouth Ophelia.
He stops, makes me check our hamper for spiders,
memorabilia, fruit, wine. How asinine. Now his monologue—
the boat rocks and he goes on
pulling those oars. Fiddle-dee-dee. . .

Peering over, I write *Vivian Mary* on water.
The lake feels bottomless from here.
If we tipped, we'd disappear, like stones.
I take an apple and consider it. —*Ow!* My tooth!
Something small falls in. Not to be outdone,
Larry yells about a splinter in his palm.
The pain's woken us both.
What a pair we are. Look how far
the shore. And now we must row.

What Rita Hayworth Threw Away

Everything's frozen: the sky, the North Sea. Me.
I am all cocoon. My red hair
so many swoon over, hidden,
and I am myself again, a woman
pacing the promenade in Aberdeen,
unnoticed, unseen.
                    Here's a locket: inside,
my old brown life, where I waited my turn
to dance with my father. *Margarita*, he calls.
I'm under the lights. Someone plucks at my hairline,
erasing what was so unwanted, take on this new life.
Forget the girls who wait. Before I turn to stone,
I drop it in the foam. Borne along—it's gone.

Something freezes on my cheek.

Nin Andrews

Nin Andrews is the author of several books including *The Book of Orgasms, Why They Grow Wings, Any Kind of Excuse, Midlife Crisis with Dick and Jane, Dear Professor, Do You Live in a Vacuum?, Sleeping with Houdini*, and *Southern Comfort*. Visit her blog:
www.ninandrewswriter.blogspot.com
and her website: www.ninandrews.com

Acknowledgments

"Southern Comfort" and "Bathing in Your Brother's Bathwater" appear in *Southern Comfort* (CavanKerry Press)
"Why I Love Angelina" appears in *Nano Fiction*
"Your Last Orgasm" appears in *DMQ Review*

Why I Love Angelina

On the island where I grew up, all the women look like Angelina Jolie. The women like to call themselves Angelina in honor of the real Angelina Jolie. Many say that Angelina is their cousin, their niece, their long-lost child. Like Angelina, they all have hair the color of crow's wings, and their lips are fat from centuries of sucking mollusks from the sand. Their hair smells of seaweed, their skin of low tide. Occasionally one of our women is born with webbed feet and hands. They swim for long hours in the ocean, catch fish with their open mouths, and dive forty feet down for conchs and oysters and rare anemones. Like Angelina, all our women are fertile, so fertile that a single woman can populate an entire village. Some are said to have populated entire nations. Even if they have no children of their own, the women adopt them. They adopt lost souls, too: street children, dogs, cats, pigeons, dolphins. And the sharks who swim close to taste the blood when it flows freely from between their swimming legs, but who rarely bite our women. Yes, even the sharks are loved by our women. The women know, as only our women can, the difference between the sharks who open their mouths wide to say *I love you Angelina*, and the sharks who are too hungry to know the difference between dinner and love.

Southern Comfort

Whiskey on the rocks. That was my dad's evening drink. As a girl, I liked to hold my father's glass, feel the cold against my face, then lift it up so I could see the light coming through the liquid, golden like the hairs on my father's arms, like Triscuits and the meadow that stretched out behind the barn. Sometimes I'd sip it, and if Mom was out of town, Dad would serve me my own drink, mixing lemon, sugar, whiskey and water, letting me taste the fire on my tongue, throat, and deep inside. *Does it burn you, Daddy?* No, he'd say. Not with just one drink. Then he'd pour himself another one *to take the edge off the day*. And I'd watch it happen, the edges of the day dissolving, everything that had been the day moving away from us, no longer true or obvious like the black and white of the clock hands moving towards bedtime. When at last it was dark and late, and all that was left were two pools of lamplight, tiny 40 watt islands, just for us, my father reading on the couch, me on my belly, head cocked sideways, staring at picture books I'd read a thousand times, I'd play a game in my mind, trying to hold on to that moment, make it last, just a little longer, and pretend, this is all there is. Just this, this whiskey light, the two of us alone, together, on a summer night.

Bathing in Your Brother's Bathwater

Bathing, Miss De Angelo informed us in health class,
is very important, especially once you become a teenager.
In fact I can smell many of you this very day,
so I advise every one of you girls
to go home and take a good long bath tonight.
I know some of your folks like to skimp on water,
but consider it homework.
Say Miss De Angelo assigned it to you.
But Girls, let me warn you.
Never take a bath in the same water as your teenage brother.
Why?
Well picture this:
all those tiny bubbles settling on your legs
when you sit in a nice tub of water.
If you could count every itty, bitty bubble,
that would be only a fraction of how many sperm
stream from a single man.
Even if he doesn't touch himself,
the water does.
And it only takes one.
One fast moving whip-tailed sperm.
And you know how easy it is to catch a cold,
how quickly that little virus races clear through you.
And once that happens,
no one will believe you're any Virgin Mary,
no matter what you say.

Your Last Orgasm

It's true, Love. The capacity for disaster is within each of us. We know this as a fact we fear and never admit. We could all fall suddenly from grace. The divine would only sigh and watch, just as I watched you walk out the door and into the winter night. Afterwards I saw my fears rise around me like a luminous cloud, like foreboding, like unrequited love and regret, like all the spoken and unspoken sorrows between us, so many of them, they had no choice but to resort to a breathless silence, first lifting of their own accord, the way the prayers of the dying rise in one last breath before sinking down, flattening into meaningless threads, a million and one disconnected thoughts, nonsequitors, each an open admission that life or beauty has no meaning after all, that from now until eternity it will always be four o'clock in the afternoon, hours before dinner and hours after our last interesting thought. That time of day when all humans begin to wonder if they will ever make love again.

They never will. This much I know, now that you have left me.

Betsy Aoki

Elizabeth (Betsy) Aoki completed her MFA at the University of Washington. She has received grants from the City of Seattle, and fellowships from the Artist Trust Foundation and the Jackstraw Writers Program. She was a finalist for the 2008 *Comstock Review's* Muriel Craft Bailey award. Her publications include the chapbook, *Every Vanish Leaves Its Trace* by Finishing Line press, inclusion in the Asian American female poets anthology *Yellow as Turmeric, Fragrant as Cloves*, and in journals such as *Dislocate, Phoebe, Poetry East, Seattle Review, Poetry Northwest, Calyx, Asian Pacific Journal*, and the *Hawai'i Pacific Review*.

Ode to the tampon

after Yusef Komunyakaa's "Ode to the Maggot"

Sister to the sweet hitachi
magic wand, bright daughter
of the moon's sly wane
there's no slipping round

your cotton necessity. Yes, you
are the warm spongy tongue
pregnant with ending, red torpedo
that keeps women swimming

through pool after pool. Bullet-headed,
flowering, you keep the best jeans
pristine, white panties without doubt.
O guardian of secret thankfulness

murmured in women's locker rooms, outlawed
in the men's, there is nothing that can change
a woman more than to be without
your easy thrust with strings attached.

Everything around us opens with time

1.
Yes, everything around us opens
with time. Feel it in the tug
at the end of the runway. Always
a last part of a plane about to leave
the ground feels the catch—
the final drag and exhale.
Then plastic cups wet gin
into the sky and out the portals
we see the curve over the wind-carved ocean.
Below us, unseen, the city sparks the city.

2.
The buildings are all square-cornered lies.
Like yeses, all the windows blink as a mood streams
out of that air box into newly cupped hands,
central parks, open carts. I've met more people
in orange sunglasses that all turned out
to be me, lost, with maps in their hands.
Smiling and waving we become each train
of thought leaving empty track in its wake.
Steel and rubber intentions always leave the platform
under swaying feet, while out windows hands palm the welcoming air—
only to release it in goodbye after goodbye. Over and over
the metal wheels sing their songs of open skies
and subjugated prairie (because everything around us
opens, in time) and so golden, we whistle our lives
defiant in the rushing dark.

Uluru, Northern Territory, Australia

The red earth sticks. I pour it out of my sandals;
it rusts my socks and coats my hands, lashes, lips.
Around us flies dive bomb us, shattering equilibrium out of our skin,
our good posture, all those elegant adjectives meaning a cold drink
after a hot day, and a long stark night to think about
how bright the stars are. How we can only see three of Jupiter's moons
out of more than sixty, cobalt and obsidian-edged spheres like marbles
in a telescope wider than my head. The guide shows us how
to dig up grubs with more protein than Wagyu beef, the tiniest
of leaves off a plant, shows us bark grown for scorching. Native peoples
captured lizards with blue tongues, used fire to drive out poisonous snakes,
with dead wood that flamed too hot in summer. They knew
the only way to live in a land like this is to burn, and burn again.

Elizabeth Austen

Elizabeth Austen is the author of *Every Dress a Decision* (Blue Begonia Press, 2011) and the chapbooks *The Girl Who Goes Alone* (Floating Bridge Press, 2010) and *Where Currents Meet* (one of four winners of the 2010 Toadlily Press chapbook award and part of the quartet *Sightline*). She produces poetry-related programming for NPR affiliate KUOW 94.9 and works as a communications specialist at Seattle Children's Hospital, where she also offers retreats and journaling workshops for the staff.
www.elizabethausten.wordpress.com

Acknowledgments

"Ebbing Hour" and "From Dr. Schnarch's Married People's Sex Manual" appear in *Every Dress a Decision* (Blue Begonia Press, 2011)

Also, every line of "From Dr. Schnarch's Married People's Sex Manual" is pilfered from *Passionate Marriage: Keeping Love & Intimacy Alive in Committed Relationships* by David Schnarch, PhD.

From Dr. Schnarch's Married People's Sex Manual

Orgasm: your brains fall out.
Having a neocortex is a liability

if you want to be a sex machine.
Low-level anxiety is why sexual

novelty can be so enticing.
Normal marital sadism:

It turns vitriol
into lubrication.

Where's your head during sex?
Couples who don't play

with each other's genitals often
play with each other's

minds instead. When
was the last time

you felt that
with your partner?

Surgeon

The person who slices past your layers
and peers into the crowded
cavern of guts knows you
in a way you will never know yourself. What if
there was nothing memorable—
your disease no worse than average, your
organs ordered and sized in the standard-issue style. Maybe

the one person who's really *seen* you
won't even remember you, couldn't distinguish
your interior from your sister's. What then? And

what about that surgeon and all those
forgotten intimacies? What kind of person
calmly cuts open another—even with good
intentions and a plan to leave things tidy
when he goes? Who carries
that kind of confidence in his hands?

For your part, admit it, weren't you
underdressed and inattentive—
sleeping, in fact, when the encounter
occurred? Oblivious to the audience
in formal attire—assistants and onlookers
leaning over the orchestra pit
of your abdomen—strings, percussion
and woodwinds tuning
at the maestro's instruction? You know

he's not going to call you later—
just the one follow-up
to ensure nothing was left behind, no
unintended consequences. Healed and whole
face it, you're no longer of interest. He's already
preparing for the next performance.

What's Done Cannot Be Undone

A stick, slow burn, the needle withdrawn.
He extracts the small mass
presses gauze to the blood. Imprisoned

in a dish, the insurgent
awaits transport. Technicians will interrogate:
investigate size, infrastructure

intent. The bandage against my breast.
Anesthetic recedes. The secret ambitions
of the body revealed. Mine, merely

the occupier's prerogative:
supply or withhold food, water, sleep.
The slip, the plot, the coup—

I can organize no defense. Who
is guilty of this
outright revolt? The little spot—

there's knocking at the gate—
silent under the microscope's
white light.

Ebbing Hour
after Kunitz

Don't offer opiates.
Lay me naked in earth's
liquid lap. Oh
lay me in the ocean's hammock
still awake enough
to know myself her own.
Feet on her salt pillow
hands at last with nothing
to grasp. For once I'll
face unblunted
an event's full force.
I don't want to miss
the last important thing
I'll ever do. Let those
friends who remain
wade out with me
beyond the breakers and push.
I want to ride the swell.

Lana Hechtman Ayers

Lana Hechtman Ayers, originally from New York, now lives in Kingston, Washington after a seventeen year sojourn in New England. She has been writing poetry since she could hold a crayon and was recently bitten by the fiction bug. Her two most recent poetry collections, *What Big Teeth* (chapbook) and *A New Red* (full-length), are concerned with the real adult life of Red Riding Hood and associates. Lana runs two poetry chapbook presses, Concrete Wolf (national) and MoonPath Press (dedicated to Pacific Northwest Poets). Ice cream is Lana's favorite food group. www.LanaAyers.com

Acknowledgments

"While the Bathtub is Filling" and "The Toe" appear in *Dance From Inside My Bones* (Snake Nation Press, 2007)

While The Bathtub Is Filling

The mirror reports that I am starting to
resemble my mother, the way she looked

that time I went into her bedroom without knocking,
saw her breasts: two weighted-down plastic bags,

bloated, slow-swinging pendulums.
I decided right then to die at eighteen,

in the prime of perkiness and elasticity.
Last year, my mother showed me a fat scar

where her left breast used to be.
It looked as if a red snake slithered

out of her heart and hid his head
in the brush of her armpit.

The longer I stared, the more I recognized
the creature above her belly for what is was: life.

Nothing about nakedness was ever that lovely.
My mother's survived this halving,

that scar, a red brooch of honor
making me proud to be a woman like her.

In a moment, when the tub is finally full,
I'll forget the mirror, all these musings,

lie back in the pale green bath,
and feel the warm water work its magic,

making buoyant, bobbing apples
of my two old gals.

The Toe

Despite how mystically moonlight snakes a path across the lake tonight, and because love is the property solely of country music, and since Plath's bell jar of pain runneth over for all eternity, I will write only of a toe—a plain enough thing—the fourth toe on my mother's right foot and how each day, despite my bathing it, my application of greasy salve, the wrapping and rewrapping to apply just enough pressure, it continued to blacken, the toe like a banana past sweetness to the other side of neglect, or salt beef dried to jerky, tenderness abandoned to gristle, so I write this about my mother's toe, how the doctor tells us it must go as if speaking of an ingrown hair or a splinter, as if it were nothing important, nothing a person spent her whole life walking on, on grass, over damp-mopped kitchen linoleum, dancing backwards in high heels over slick-waxed ballroom floors, or in babyhood grabbed for all googly-eyed and occasionally even sucked, this dried-up toe that oddly causes mother no pain, and yet when the doctor says the toe must go, this woman who was a marble column at father's bedside during his failed chemo, who later presided over father's grave, stolid as a granite headstone, and not long after, this woman who sat composed as Rodin's "Bather" as another doctor spoke the word mastectomy to her, and all through radiation wore a Mona Lisa smile, this woman does a thing I'd never seen her do, my mother cries, sobs, weeps, exhausts all the tissues in the doctor's stainless dispenser, and keeps crying over this very small rotten toe, this calamity of losing what one least expected to lose.

Dorothy Barresi

Dorothy Barresi is the author of four books of poetry: *American Fanatics* (University of Pittsburgh Press, 2010), *Rouge Pulp, The Post-Rapture Diner*, winner of an American Book Award, and *All of the Above*. She is the recipient of two Pushcart Prizes, the Emily Clark Balch Prize, and a Fellowship from the National Endowment for the Arts. She is Professor of English and Creative Writing at California State University, Northridge. She lives in Los Angeles.

Acknowledgments

"Welles after *Kane*" appears in *Malpais Review*
"Vegan Heaven" appears in *PoetryMagazine.com* (titled "Pro-Union")

Admit One

You're the poet laureate of privacy, my husband said.
I wasn't ignoring him, I was reading a book.
You blim the blam of privacy,

you skin privacy's fruit.
Yeah, my son said. If privacy needed a guide dog
you'd be its trainer. You'd help privacy sniff its own butt.

That's nonsensical, I said.
I could tell without looking he was proud of that one.
I'm in this family, aren't I?

I'm right here in the living room.
But if your body turned up
at the corner of First & Homicide, my husband said, you'd come back to blow away

the chalk. Admit it—you're a pupa;
you haven't eaten your way out of your little silk tent yet.
You haven't gotten off the blimp.

My stepson wanted in.
You're Santa's Village, he said, where
it's Christmas every day but closed on Christmas. Wait,

I said, wasn't that joke on *The Simpsons*?
Oh, snap, he said, I forgot:
you're privacy's ghost writer now, privacy's highly evolved

groupie slash divorce lawyer slash
salt water aquarium.
Does privacy take one lump or two?

Have you checked your municipal holdings lately?
Few and falling, I said, serene
enough with my civil disobedience,

and even, I suppose, with the fidgety loneliness I've been wrestling all my life
like a bear in a cheap roadside attraction,
though I couldn't help wondering

what was the seed and what the ground?
Why, when I could redeem myself
with a simple open act,

was I always weighing the hearts of the dead? And why—
when temporarily exhausted by *that* exercise—
did I guard myself as though I'd found

black box proof of faulty wiring
and a survival sermon whispered on emergency frequencies
only I should hear?

Ho, ho, ho. I'm not listening, I said, flipping pages, not reading now but imagining
how it might be accomplished:
a casual, unchecked nature.

Not scout, sniff, private dick,
comptroller, CEO-embalmer of every unrehearsed word.
Whatever happens after that, happens. The hell with it—

stop minding my own business!
I let the idea
take me to the movies. I held its hand in the easeful dark. I closed my eyes.

Who wants popcorn? my husband said, giving up.
If privacy were extinct, my son said, kissing my cheek, you'd be deader
than the passenger pigeon and the Carolina parakeet.

Vegan Heaven

The waiting room is hot.
The plastic upholstery is slick, the tunnel out,

into what's owed you, long and
paved with antennae, eye-globes on stalks, gaudy multiple
mouthparts & the odd red etceteras

of every bug
you've ever crushed since you first fell

toddling
into your mother's arms

(she thought she'd *feel* more, seeing that. Never mind.
She was an early hippie and stoned).

We are all gods to what we kill.

Redemption's light is chained—one overhead
incandescent, mega high watt.
Wait a sec, you say, to the intake crone bent

on shoving you forward
toward what,
an apology or an altar call?

A nonesuch healing?
I saved cows and pigs and fish
with faces, I didn't eat the elephants in circuses—I ruined more than one kid's

happycircus with my howling
demonstration
I'll have you know.

Perfect, she says, keep moving.
Into the glop! The filament feelers!
And a buzz-saw *swoon swoon* from every

cockroach-junebug-sweater moth that dared
jumble at your torn mosquito screens:

The Destroyer, come back for them at last!

To not know
and *still* have cared—

would that have been the way to go?
Thank-you, a lint-lithe wasp

stings, weeping in your ear.
Thank you, thank you, thank you.

Welles after *Kane*

Potential: a glass novelty containing a miniature American snowfall falling

into lapovers, melds, segues of thought and super-
numerary language
shot directly into blazing arcs,
disappointment's long dissolve.

The film is never commercially released.
The film is sometimes, although rarely, commercially released.
The film is ever

scrapped, scenes re-shot, false noses
fashioned from mortuary wax—

Welles doing *all* the voices this time!

(Falstaff, gutted, selling ignoble wine).

Variety reports:
"Instead of not making two pics for RKO, he'll not make five."

There's little gravy in it, the artist admits,
but the movie in his head
is perfect.

Judith Barrington

Judith Barrington is the author of three collections of poetry including *Horses and the Human Soul*, selected by The Oregon State Library for "150 Books for the Sesquicentennial." Her *Lost Lands* recently won the Robin Becker Chapbook Award. *Lifesaving: A Memoir* won the 2001 Lambda Book Award and was a finalist for the PEN/Martha Albrand Award for the Art of the Memoir. She is also the author of the bestselling *Writing the Memoir: From Truth to Art* and is a faculty member of the University of Alaska, Anchorage's low-residency MFA Program. She teaches workshops in Britain and Spain. www.judithbarrington.com

Windrowing

And here she comes: the girl I used to be
with her stick legs shamefully lacking curves,
squatting in her grass hut's musty air,
its woven stems a trellis of light and dark.
It's the smell that ushers her in—the itching too:
not just the hut but overnight pony camp,
sleeping in a barn with bats and whispered tales
of a howling, headless, galloping ghost,
insects with legs creeping along her back—
real at first but then imagined till dawn.

She drops in casually towing behind her
the smooth-running sled of decades, piled high
with clear and certain memories of hay:
huts and barns, stables full of horses
chomping, grinding, absent-mindedly swallowing
bale after bale of fescue, timothy, oat,
alfalfa, clover and pea—sliced from a meadow
with blades of steel, spread and dried,
baled and tied with hairy twine that she cut
with her sharp Toledo knife, then separated,
seeds flying like motes through rays of sun
as she shook them back to freedom.

Here she comes, stepping from trees that sigh,
a revenant forgetting about her legs—
at least until the day she spreads them out
in tall grasses with some boy—but all she remembers
now are the chest-high, wind-blown walls of green
and the flattened circle the two of them leave behind
as if a horse had stretched out there
for a long sleep in the poppy-scented sun.

Breath

At first I thought her breath was sweet—
maybe just because it was hers:
sometimes a trace of mint below
the antiseptic tang that wafted from
her lips, her tongue, all her body's skin.
I breathed it in.

Chanel Number 5 could not disguise
the enigmatic whiff that trailed behind
when she made an entrance, eloquent hand outstretched.
I watched her dab the scent behind each ear
as she sat in front of the triple mirror
catching my eager eye.

At first I thought the van that delivered
a heavy crate to the back door twice a week
came from Dai the grocer, except that the driver,
a lad in a sheepskin coat, looked furtive—
and why were there never rice krispies or cheese
or bread in the breadbox?

The day I caught her stashing the vodka up high
behind the teapot, well out of sight,
she fell down the stairs in the middle of the night.
I found her there, a heap of bones,
and carried her, moaning, back up to bed—
her breath still hers, still sweet.

Elegy for a Green Convertible

My mother was old enough to know better—
or so I thought at the time. But what could I know

of her joy as I raced south on the narrow road,
my mother dead, her Triumph held tight between

my careless hands. Poplars swished by,
rhythmic shadows snapping across my eyes.

Hypnotized from Normandy to Spain,
I tailed a man in a Daimler Dart, both of us

four-wheel-drifting the hairpin bends and flirting
along the straights till I entered my movie:

I was the star but the ending was always bad...
Of course, I should have cared for it better:

it would have been a sign of respect for god's sake
to nurse, even to polish its sun-bleached paintwork.

But I neglected it just as we all neglected
the two old dogs, lost without mother's sweet talk.

Now I think it was a crime; but back then
I double-clutched and skinned my inherited tires.

Somewhere in a graveyard that Triumph lies—
stripped of its seats, its wheels, its lights,

an iron skeleton, rust-circles blooming
while beetles cross and recross my mother's bones.

Mary Biddinger

Mary Biddinger is the author of three collections of poetry: *Prairie Fever* (Steel Toe Books, 2007), the chapbook *Saint Monica* (Black Lawrence Press, 2011), and *O Holy Insurgency* (Black Lawrence Press, 2012), and co-editor of one volume of criticism: *The Monkey and the Wrench: Essays into Contemporary Poetics* (U Akron Press, 2011). Her poems have appeared or are forthcoming in numerous magazines, including *Copper Nickel, Devil's Lake, Gulf Coast, The Iowa Review, Ploughshares*, and *Puerto del Sol*. She teaches literature and creative writing at The University of Akron/NEOMFA, and edits *Barn Owl Review*, the *Akron Series in Poetry*, and the *Akron Series in Contemporary Poetics.*
www.marybiddinger.com

The Business of It

At a certain point I began to wonder
what the springs in the mattress thought
of us. Whether there was somebody

in there, keeping track. They'd set all
the racehorses free weeks earlier.
My body learned not to register thunder

as something beyond a disruption.
Asleep with my head on your shoulder,
it seemed fitting that the mares left

last. My own fingers demonstrated how.
You asked if it was a detonation,
or more like the euphoria of black ants

crawling one by one into a straw.
Their exodus the opposite of our bed's
migration. And what about clocks

left gutted on a sawhorse, gold entrails.
Who could trust them again, once
the gears were subjected to daylight?

No answers from the stable boy,
pitching bales into the chipper at dawn.
When they hauled our old mattress

away, they promised it would become
a haven for orphaned magpies.
Even the stitching would be unstitched

in the name of conservation. How
dreadful, you said. And our bed inched
across the last remaining pasture.

Fortitude

As in: there's no backside to a shadow.

An engine cried all night and woke us.

Who could stop its shudders if not you?

We were well within the limits by law.

I am not referencing bylaws, just walls

to rattle against. They never grow old.

Paint creeps them inward by decade.

I once lived in a cabinet without doors.

It took years to coax you in. Countless

wet blackberries balanced in my palm.

Two meanings to signify *manipulation*.

I favored the latter, and fortified myself.

It's easier than you'd think, ascension.

I used to believe it was not meant for me.

We should've looked at the clock to note

an exact moment of revelation, trained

the bells to sound its daily anniversary.

All I remember is that it was freezing.

A stranger walked into a windowpane

as if nothing had happened. No pigeons

chastised the blue awnings. Our bravery

so warm that no room could contain us.

A Coronation

I belong in the second category,
hammered into the siding along
with all the other nails, only
this one made it clear through,
and alleluia. Now untie me
so we can parade the avenues.
The restless patients all waving
their tentacles in our direction.
We were so ready for fireworks
we hushed in the closet and lit
just a couple of them. And now
the entire neighborhood's ablaze.
I brought my hot glue gun along
since we had nothing on a leash.
The matching straw hats clearly
too much, but that didn't deter us
from passing them to strangers.
We refused to honor the street
definition of *chronic*. Youthful
defiance was best demonstrated
by my mouth's insubordination
in times of dire panic. Translated:

no measure to calculate the drift
of my lips down your back. If ships
were alive they would drive west
into the gray of an afternoon only
meant to bisect us. A ship within
a ship. Outside we found the deck
and an anchor rope. We begged to
dive in, even if the sea was green.
The only backdrop in sight: brick
and the leavening grit to pin brick
upon brick. I made just one point
that night when pressed against
the length of your body. Neither
of us asleep yet, one frog outside
waiting for a reply to its queries.
You said the trees were desperate,

or else why would they stand that
still. I told you they'd been moving
the same way for a thousand years.

An Incarnation

Sorrow? And what for?
After everything's expunged

we'll be teeth in the teapot,
throwing orange peels

at the prophet. Detail
the inches that might exist

between us, as if anything
could. I'd issue you

the most delicious
violation ever on the books

in our county. Did it really
have *a seat?* If so,

why not consult us
for infrastructure advice

before handing grenades
to the goblins?

In the woods, you
promised to show me your

doctrine. I demonstrated my
theorem. Two magpies

coupled wildly nearby.
The tree stumps all in rows,

like lockers. We defined our
genius like we ate

our way through
every resurrection in sight.

Elizabeth Bradfield

Elizabeth Bradfield is the author of *Approaching Ice* (Persea, 2010), which was a finalist for the James Laughlin Award from the Academy of American Poets, and *Interpretive Work* (Arktoi Books, 2008), which won the 2009 Audre Lorde Prize and was a finalist for a Lambda Literary Award. In 2005, Bradfield founded the grassroots-distributed and guerilla-art-inspired *Broadsided Press* (www.broadsidedpress.org), which still runs. A former Stegner Fellow, she works as a naturalist and lives on Cape Cod. www.ebradfield.com

Acknowledgments

"Eskimo Whizzamajig" appears in *Orion Magazine*
"Misapprehensions of Nature" and "I Am Lowing" appear in *Superstition Review*
"Of Seasonality" appears in *Green Mountains Review*

Misapprehensions of Nature

That crows plant acorns, twist
them into soil, properly spaced,
to serve as future roosts.

That bees are improper
because they have a queen
no king, and manta rays

wrap divers in the dark
blankets (*mantilla*)
of their wings.

That dolphins
love us, that deer love us,
and the kit brought in and given milk

is just as happy. That we can know
what it is for a fox
to be happy.

~

Two men bought a lion
at Harrods, reared it
in their small apartment.

Released it (reluctantly) to savannah.
And then, years later,
sure that it would know them,

went and called its name
into the grasses.
It ran toward them.

That they would be mauled.

That perhaps they should
be mauled. But it

tumbled them, licked their faces,

Everyone was crying.
            We were crying,
even the lion was nearly crying.

I Am Lowing

for Arctic Explorer Donald B. MacMillan

Chewing cud or
pissing into crabgrass, cows
orient their bodies toward the poles.

You're not surprised, Mac. You know what it is
to feel your iron self
pulled.

Deer, too, and other grazers
observed in fields shot by satellites
tend north/south.

I'm living in a city and it's loud.
The pole star is faint
through civic aurora.

When power lines cross herds,
animals redirect themselves
to that hummed path.

They don't mean to. Since moving here,
I've flown east/west a dozen times,
back north only once. Mac,

birds, whales, and bees align. I know
I yearn along a worn rut
in the earth's field. As you did.

I don't mind being unoriginal
in this way.

Eskimo whizzamajig

label, circa 1940 for an ivory spear tip
in the MacMillan Collection, Provincetown

Optimism, in a strange,
American way, this zippy
caption for what was foreign
beyond language.

Thingamabob. Doohickey
distant as the need
for a *haasux*
(spear-thrower in Aleut)
or *unaaq* (Inupiaq pole
to check ice thickness).

This tool (perhaps a *sakku*)
clever and useless to the secretary
(was it Miriam?) who typed
the label that has yellowed.

Widget. Whatzit. . .

but some words drift.

Take *vaxa gididzagh*, Athabaskan for
that with which things are spread
and so now *butter knife*.
Or *lastax*—fermented fur seal flipper—
now the three-petaled gizmo
that spins beneath a boat.

And consider the kayak,
translated through fiberglass
and rotomold,
neoprene and rubber.
Bright alchemy
that's made it whizzamajig
to its own source.

Of Seasonality

Black-tailed, mule, and white-tailed—they wax.
New growth pulsed by velvet, tender, and so
summer's a season of backing. Of moving forward
through greened bramble and then backing.

They have time to adjust.
                                        They don't wake thrashing,
to realign, fitting the amended body.
confused by the weight and shape (later,
confused by its loss).

                                        I am away
again. I am bumbling, mis-weighted, strange.

Someone's proven the mind lies, at least in part,
outside the body. How far
until my mind does not rest on you?

The grown antler hardens. The not-bone
becomes not-tender, its soft fur
unnecessary. So:

Rub. Rub.
                                        A tree now gone
                                                            of bark in one
                                                  raw spot, pale
          and hurt and beautiful in the dark wood.

Then bellow & clatter. Bend & posture.
And the valleys echo or moss takes the sound.
Soon they're shed of weight which
even while splendid was burden,
and at last that season's done.

Ronda Broatch

Ronda Broatch is the author of *Shedding Our Skins*, (Finishing Line Press, 2008) and *Some Other Eden,* (2005). Nominated several times for the Pushcart, Ronda is the recipient of a 2007 Artist Trust GAP Grant, and is currently the Poetry Editor for *Crab Creek Review*.

Dangerous

Days when what I've done
and not done waxes raw
as a burn I coddle
under my tongue, in my breast
pocket, palm of my hand
on the steering wheel.
Times like these I indulge
myself, dim my eyes a brief
moment, trusting road and other
drivers. I close them
for seconds that widen
into minutes
my little dark place of forgetting
as I climb the hill toward my son's
school. If I don't move
a muscle, take deep
and measured breaths
my eyelids pressed like altar linens, I can write
while driving, sleep
while writing, the road
lengthening into days, breaths
deepening into months. A few years
of this and—who knows?
I may arrive at nirvana
or at least my son's school
in one piece
before crossing the solid
double yellow, the nebulous
void where everything worth shutting
your eyes for
disappears like socks in the dryer
like a burn must
after so much time.

Dangerous, Again

makes plans for the future
Dangerous agrees

to leaving   if only for a week
Dangerous sees red

in your eyes
feels tall   impossibly

small.
Unhinged

it watches the chemo drip   misses
blips in the body's tête-à-tête

It says let's sleep
often   exclaims

there will be good days ahead   this course of drugs
will fix   carry you well into the next twenty years

says remission
Dangerous believes all this

thumbs its teeth against the odds
fingers crossed behind its back

Because You Are Dying, and Other Excuses

I confess that I have been less
than I:
less mother, daughter, wife.
I confess

I've forgotten to pay
the quarterly taxes, attention
to the larger particulars. I confess

that I have turned off my phone.
Turned it on only
when guilt rang,
            and

            I confess to the cookbook
I'd rather read than bake a cake, make
lasagna with pesto, confess to

the checkbook I'd rather siesta
than shop for gifts for the birthday
            we'll celebrate, three days
late.

I confess to the eggs in the pan
                                    forgotten in the pan
                        (forgotten in the pan)
            long the pan

blackened, the eggs
a shell
of their former selves. I confess

to the trash bin that accepted
these two small murders without question
the air confessing my transgressions

my never-enough
my less-than.

This Is The House That Grief Built

with sagging breasts and room
for questioning God. A closet

of loss, sanctuary for the daughter
gone a week, armchair of the father
soon to be. Black hole

of Holy Ghost.
Years, the years the mother
wasn't a mother so much

as a phone call, an obligation
in black on the green hall table,
Thursday nights at eight.

This house has teeth and valises.
This house has chutes and blast cells.
This house will take in strays

the father collects, his obsessions
filling corners until he can barely
breathe. This house will breathe

for him when he leaves, the mother
shelved, a reliquary, an hour-
glass empty and filling again.

Gloria Burgess

Gloria Burgess's poetry celebrates the spiritual and evocative oral traditions of her ancestry. Her poetry appears in diverse publications, including *The Ringing Ear: Black Poets Lean South, Gathering Ground, The Open Door*, and *Journey of the Rose*. Gloria begins her latest book, *Dare to Wear Your Soul on the Outside*, with the touching story of her father's life-changing relationship with Nobel Laureate William Faulkner, weaving in threads of inspirational poetry, narrative, and reflections.
www.gloriaburgess.com

Acknowledgments

"The Open Door" appears in *The Open Door* (book); *ColorsNW Magazine*, and *This Should Be Enough* (anthology)

Note on "Sanctuary" from the poet: *William Faulkner, Nobel Prize and Pulitzer Prize winning author, was my father's benefactor. Faulkner paid for my father to attend college at a time when he had few prospects of earning enough money to pay for it himself. This was Faulkner's way of dismantling institutionalized racism long before desegregation was mandated in the South; it was my father's way of freeing himself and his family from the strictures of apartheid.*
"Sanctuary" appears in *The Ringing Ear: Black Poets Lean South* (anthology) and *Gathering Ground* (anthology)

The Open Door

for my ancestors and our children

i wasn't there   i didn't stand at the threshold
of the open door   my back wasn't wracked
beneath a ceiling so low even children lay prone
my spirit wasn't riven   i wasn't cowed
bloodied   shamed   no one stripped me
of my name   i wasn't there   i wasn't at Goreé
or anywhere along that shore

i was born inside the golden door
and i'm here by grace standing on the shoulders
of women and men stout in spirit fierce in soul
and oh by the blessed sanctity of God
though i wasn't hounded through that open door
or driven to cross a merciless sea i still
have the sting of salt in my soul nightmares
of a watery grave   i still search furtively
for signs of my tribe   outstretched hands   a cool
drinka water calabash smile   i still tread softly
muted by the glare of ghostly strangers   i still push back
the rising bile when a glassy-eyed elder looks too long
or wide   i've learned to question all kinds of kings
to stand firm on the laps of queens   some days
i can't tell the difference and fall to my knees
dragged down by the tide all over again

Sanctuary

for William Faulkner and my father, Earnest McEwen, Jr.

Between the brush of angels' wings
and furious hooves of hell, two mortal men
fell down. How you must have looked—
white shirt stained, khakis fatigued,
smelling of sweat and smoke,
hair at odds with itself and the world.
At the threshold among your restless dead
in echo and shadow of ancient oaks,
providing sanctuary, offering shade,
you had many worlds behind you,
few yet to be born: stories of insurgence,
scorn, decay—theme and variations
of a vanquished South.

Leaning against a jamb
of antebellum brass, you watched, waited,
raised weary arm and hand, saluted
the familiar stranger. *Come. Enter. Sit. Sing.*

You reached each other across the grate.
What you two must have known of heaven and hell.

Jill Crammond

Jill Crammond is a poet/artist/mother, funding her poetry passion by teaching children's art and poetry classes. Her work has appeared in *Crab Creek Review, Boxcar Poetry Review, Weave, qarrtsiluni* and others. She is a contributor to *Poets' Quarterly* and co-founder of the online poetry community Big Tent Poetry. She occasionally blogs about life as a (newly single) mom-poet at www.jillypoet.wordpress.com

All the Pretty Mothers

I don't even want to look at you.
And suddenly I am that mother—
cigarette hanging by a slice of lip
hip thrust into the door jamb,
blood-shot eyes drooping
with the weight of yesterday's mascara.

It is morning in the gingerbread house
and no-one has eaten the children yet.

The pretty mothers, already at the bus stop,
guard their children and gawk,
fall back on well-heeled urban myths:

Their pretty mommy was abducted by aliens.
See? That boy and girl didn't do what they were told.
Their mommy turned into a witch
and now she's going to eat them.

I want these children to eat me
out of house and home.
I have laced the curtains with licorice
replaced the window panes with spun sugar
strung twinkle lights hung with gummy bears from the ceiling.

I want to run from this fairy tale in flip flops or shit-kickers
because if you haven't figured it out by now
I am not the mother in sensible shoes.

So, After Thirty Years of Wilting Lilies, June Cleaver Decides to Resurrect the Garden, or: June Cleaver Has Designs on the Landscaper, Finds Gardening Is a Passion She Can Really Believe In

What have you done with my dog?
she asks the gardener, planting
her feet in the new grass between the man
and his shears. She does not fear sharp edges

not the rib she curled around last night
not the mouth of the cave she searched
this morning for her dog. Lost.
She kicks a pile of dead lilies

blesses the cloud of choking pollen
fertility is a messy business
thrusting seeds deep into
fallow ground, spring after spring

soon she will tire of shrugging
claiming the soil is sandy
the pine trees acidic
the sun angry with her patch of land.

Believe it when she says it is the plants
she speaks of, green that mocks her.
Man, what have you done with my dog?
Where have you taken his body?

She is one of the many, the flock who call
their dog their own, flesh and blood, brother, own.
Late at night she walks to the garden
relieves herself around the perimeter

keep the deer out, keep the hare out.
Each morning she peels sun like a cloak
from dirt-streaked cheek. Rubs moon
from her eyes. Fallen asleep in the beds

again. Using her whole body
to root the seeds. *Where is my dog?*
The gardener—key to the growing
if only she could get her hands on him.

He is walking backwards, sowing a trail.

How We Finally Made it Out of Oz

It was the year of the crumbling castle
tornadoes at every turn.
Our home tumbled
around us, the brick I laid
so carefully
turning to webs of straw
and me with no silver loom to weave
our sorry band of lions, tigers and bears
into something like a poppy field
or a brick road,
roots swelling beneath mud and gold.

You know how it is when you wake
from a dream, the strain of a banjo
(violin if you're lucky) staining the morning
fooling you into believing the best way out
is to find the eye and hurl yourself into the disaster?

You know the epilogue to the Wizard of Oz?
The one no one has ever seen
where the little man turns everyone into zombies
who watch wicked Dorothy slip out of her ruby shoes
roll striped stockings up one pale leg at a time,
follow her down that sticky black tar road?

When the castle showed itself to be nothing
more than a poorly drawn barn
when at last it fell to its clapboard knees,
that's when I packed the children
and myself into a glass valise
and we finally saw the way out.

Barbara Crooker

Barbara Crooker's work has appeared in magazines as diverse as *Yankee, The Christian Science Monitor, Highlights for Children*, and *The Journal of American Medicine* (JAMA). She is the recipient of the 2006 Ekphrastic Poetry Award from Rosebud, the 2004 WB Yeats Society of New York Award, the 2003 Thomas Merton Poetry of the Sacred Award, and three Pennsylvania Council on the Arts Creative Writing Fellowships. Her books are *Radiance*, which won the 2005 Word Press First Book competition and was a finalist for the 2006 Paterson Poetry Prize, *Line Dance*, (Word Press 2008), which won the 2009 Paterson Award for Literary Excellence, and *More* (C & R Press, 2010).
www.barbaracrooker.com

Acknowledgments

"Owl Hour" appears in *Tar River Poetry*
"Sugar" appears in *Poet Lore*
"*La Neige et L'Hiver*" appears in *Off the Coast*

La Neige Et L'Hiver

after a study in acrylic, ink, & encaustic by Claire Giblin

I stretch my canvas tight as a sail,
size it with gesso, sand it down.
Apply layers of oils, wave
after wave of powdered
pigment, beeswax, melt them
with a torch. I'm trying to fix
the fog's sfumato as it speaks
in the old mother tongue:
horizon cloud sea.

~

Light, both particle and wave,
is the dark ground I'm working on,
the gouache of my mother's death.
An empty beach after the tide recedes:
ribbed sand, striations of clouds.

~

The seasons change, peel off their coats.
Grief comes and goes with its shaker of salt,
pours over me without warning. Puts items
in my grocery cart that only she would eat.

~

Everything is blurred, time folding back
on itself. My palette's a smudgy grisaille
of slate, steel, smoke. And ochre.

~

It was like morning on the first day
when she passed, land dividing
from sea, air from water, soul
from body. What remained
was a coracle, a small boat
with a canvas for its sail.

Sugar

My mother is a hungry ghost. She comes to me in dreams,
asking, where's the applesauce? The kind *you* make?
Cooked with the skins on, whirled with cinnamon
and nutmeg, swirled through a food mill, smooth fruit
separated from skins, cores, seeds. Shouldn't this sweetness
exist in the afterlife? Yet I've heard that's what angels crave
those times they're glimpsed, partly visible, a rustle of wings,
an opening in the air. Apparently, they shimmer,
made out of gossamer and light. We always long
for what we don't have, and they yearn to be incarnate,
to know the hunger of the tongue. Filaments of cotton candy,
fistfuls of sugar, the long slow drip of honey and molasses.
I tried to sweeten my mother's last days, bringing
her a deconstructed sundae—coffee ice cream in one cup,
hot fudge in another, whipped cream in a third. But her hunger
is not appeased. She still longs for this world, its confectionary
splendor. She would, if she could, open her mouth
like a bird or a baby, and let me spoon it in.

Owl Hour

I don't know why I get so cold at ten o'clock, but that's when I'm drawn,
like some sort of nightbird, to our nest upstairs in the flannel sheets,
once the color of pinot noir, now duller, patinaed by the silver
of our skins. I need to pile on the blue blanket, the heavy woolen
one from Ireland, the Broken Star quilt, before I stop
shivering. Sometimes the house itself quivers in the wind.
Then you come up, and we arrange ourselves like a nest
of measuring cups. Some of our friends now sleep alone, half
the set missing. I've told you *you're not allowed to die first;*
I don't do numbers—checkbook, taxes, bills. My breasts
press into your back; my hand with the numb fingers stretches
over your heart. How lucky we are to have found each other;
what if I hadn't gone to the party that night? The second time
for both of us; we know how it can all go wrong. Even
when I can't sleep, I listen to the hoots and calls
of your breathing, which both keeps me awake
and will be the first thing I'll miss when all the nights
are silent. We know there'll be an *afterwards*;
we're not that young anymore. I turn, and turn again,
the way a dog circles before he lies down. And though
we can't see them, the stars twirl overhead, each one nested
in the place in space it's supposed to call home.

Rachel Dacus

Rachel Dacus has published three collections of poetry, including the full-length collections *Earth Lessons* and *Femme au chapeau*, and a chapbook, *Another Circle of Delight*. Her new collection, *Gods of Water and Air*, was a semi-finalist for the 2010 Akron Poetry Prize and will be published by Kitsune Books in 2012. She has published stories, essays, reviews, and interviews, and her poems have appeared in *Atlanta Review, Boulevard, Many Mountains Moving, Prairie Schooner, Rattapallax*, and other journals. She also has a CD of poems accompanied by music, *A God You Can Dance*. She lives in Walnut Creek, California and works as a grant writer and fundraising consultant. www.dacushome.com

Acknowledgments

"Thunder-Edged" appears in *Prairie Schooner*
"Femme au chapeau" appears in *Bellingham Review*

Femme au chapeau

after a painting of his wife by Matisse, 1905

She's ready to doff tradition's muff and the cane
on which she stylishly leans. Yeats is about
to write: *The bees build in the crevices.* Her mane
of red is upswept, but wants out.
Hollowed by chaos, her face is Internet
turquoise and neon pink, cartooned as if
she were a television on which we get
the perennial game show, *What's the Dif?*
Miracles of the time are all around her—
Freud and his unconscious, Pavlov's reflex—
a patent examiner with a theory that avers
time's not absolute. Matisse goes psychedelic
on a woman's face. Titled *Woman,* like so
many painters' wives, she seems not to see
the changes or first she'd remove that chapeau,
its crushing fruit, its dour antiquity.
Eyes wild as pinwheels whirl questions:
If we can't escape birth or condition,
what's the point? If not now, when?
Who will I be, Henri, when I come to fruition?
As a woman all rainbow atomic ignition.

Thunder-Edged

Sun under chin,
she rambles after them
as they garden the hillside.
Brushed with light, she rides
low among slim stems,
thunder-edged.
Slipping through holes
in wind, she rolls
under a flower's hem.
Buttercup, they call
her, but tuck her into a null
crib to listen to thin
mosquito hours. Again
and again, no one.
The child's ear hums
with moon's footfall
on the hill, a cloud-tall
lady who kindles the lights.
By day, rolled up
tight, she is given to those
who prick her
scalp with needle fire.
She blurs and shrinks
into thickets, rooting fists on stone.
In the shimmer of alone,
she spins light, sparks flee
the first wound,
see how it brims.

Madeline DeFrees

Madeline DeFrees has published eight poetry collections, most recently *Spectral Waves* (2006). *Blue Dusk: New and Selected Poems, 1951-2001* was awarded the 2002 Lenore Marshall Poetry Prize. She's received fellowships from the Guggenheim Foundation and the NEA. In 2008, University of Washington Libraries awarded her the Maxine Cushing Gray Visiting Writers Fellowship.

Acknowledgments

"Desire Hathaway 2," "Desire Hathaway 3" and "Jenny Martinson Learns Semaphore," appear in *Crab Creek Review*
"Whaling Wives: Submit Claiborne" and "Jenny Martinson, Whaling Captain's Widow, Addresses the Historical Society" appear in *Nimrod,* Vol. 29, No. 1

from *Whaling Wives*

Desire Hathaway

2

I set up house in a timbered cranny of the ship's
cabin, my heart already
heavy with hope and his child. I would not yield
my body to his mother for delivery and answered
his every argument with wiles.
Some visitor must have reported I wear
bloomers on deck, as is my habit. The words
hung still in air when she dispatched,
posthaste, her frosty disapproval. If she were to
guess my condition, I should have little
peace. My husband insists that she must know
very soon or be unforgivably
offended. Across the wide sea, it appears, armed
truce continues, although she cannot
touch me here.

The crew is another matter, the men
satisfied with nothing
meaner than my husband's undivided passion. I see
my true rival is the Arctic Ocean.
That, and his mother's cold blood.
The one standing watch calls him from our bed
at each imagined peril. I do not quarrel with duty
but have been already widowed four years and would
be shut of that. When sailors jest about the easy
women of Talcahuano, his eyes
freeze over like hers. Can a son alter his nature?
I feel the small mouth pulling
at my breast and can believe *my* blood enough to warm
another's. I do not need the ship's glass to show me
clearly rough seas ahead.

Desire Hathaway

3

The island company he left me in was bland enough
to bore me: the wife of the consul.
One of those women who cluck and coo over their
strutting husbands. When I showed her
the dress I'd made for the child's birth, a devious
bit of embroidery of Nathan's ample,
untried handkerchief, she said it would not do.
We made our rounds of the shops, felt every bolt
of cloth, chose between lavender and

ivory, ivory and
summer yellow. Inquired the price as if the child
might wear this souvenir from the arrival day
forward. Such, the beginning. As time drew near
for my lying-in, she snipped,
tucked and gathered, starting over every morning,
Penelope besieged. When the true labor
came, I was alone for the first time,
my belly gripped by devils. I must have screamed
the door open on a witch's foul

rags, charms, and
mumbo-jumbo. Astonished, I found myself wanting
Nathan's mother! Cold, yes, but
clean as snow at the antipodes. I remember piled
sheets, fluffed towels, laundry
boiled pristine white, the fresh good smell of a godly
household. Some wild voice out of my body
tore the air, and I saw the door
swing wide again. There stood my fine British doctor,
half his fee already gone

in some dark saloon, the reek
of drink still on him. I chose against my sex.
Medical science, civilization, no matter
how depraved. Soon he had taken hold. I did
his bidding, a trussed hen reduced to obedience.
My stormy labor ended as my son's

long trial began. Stale air forced a passage through
small lungs, his cry turned pain to fierce
rejoicing. Far away, Nathan
commanded his crew,

satisfied at having made due
arrangements for my wifely comfort. If money were
all, he had provided handsomely, and no
report of near catastrophe could persuade him
otherwise. Thus, I must be
dismissed as wayward—ungrateful even—with no defense
except caprice, no witness to
the unattended terrors of this birth.

Submit Claiborne

Today the cooper has made a small coffin, sturdy
and delicate as scrimshaw. Yesterday I drew a black
line around Captain's entry in the ship's log
to honor our son. When Freddie was learning
to talk, we went ashore one time
after I had been seasick considerably and could not
walk. The carriage rattled up the cobbled
hill. Freddie grew thoughtful. He looked so serious
I had to smile when he asked, "Is *this*
Grandma's house?" not knowing it
just a hack.

Another time he threw the cook's hat
overboard and yelled "There
she breaches!" Playing zoo he shoved a peanut
up his nose and had to be taken to
grumpy Doctor Fowler. That's done. I made a little
wreath of geranium leaves and a white
slip of handkerchief silk for the pillow. Rough water
put a hawser on last night. Today, the surface
calm. I do not approve of Sunday whaling, but they go
all the same, leave me below deck

to distract myself.
Soon, the crew will be cutting in, and the stench,
more than I can bear, although I must. This morning
our cockatoo ate copper and died. Nathan
could not build a wall, but he made a wide chalk mark
to keep the children safe. Stay *here*, it reminded
Laura on the *Splendid* deck, and her toes
brushed the line. Not Freddie. He crossed and crossed
again every time he thought
no one was looking.

Worked on the Log Cabin quilt
in weak light. Too many pieces
cut from *his* cloth. That time the deckhand set a fire
among the shooks, my hands trembled
seven days. We had to save the food, so Nathan used
an ax to break open the hold. Every morsel I ate

smoke brought back the shaking. The naked black who came
aboard in the Sooloo Sea was not
so fearful. Our hens keep dying off, our cat a skeleton
or apology for one.

Small help from my Bible. I cannot
make Freddie an angel climbing up and down
Jacob's Ladder. I see him thrown upon the tender
mercies of the deep. We had four pigs. One
drowned in hot fat. Laura found the first waterspout
this morning. She wants to keep Fred's place
at table. Just now she brought a string of pressed
flowers—black-eyed susans from our
stay in Talcahuano, Sailor's Heaven.

Even when the ship
leaked 2500 strokes a day, we hoped to preserve
our precious cargo. The men cheered when Ladder Hill
came into view, and we limped
timely into port, rudder, keel and shoe torn away.

Jenny Martinson Learns Semaphore

This morning the morning watch killed the Ox
the wild horny one we got in Borneo. It tasted
quite nice next to weeks of salt
as Cook prepared fresh meat for Captain's table.
Steward throwed most all
teaspoons overboard with the dishes water in one
Callous throw. We take turnabout
now. Our black Hen was not spared as she flew
leeward, very soon Eat by two large
Birds. On deck I see how everything happens
talking with the Flags. When a Brig yesterday
hove to, I pick out Answers
from a Book which we have. It looks odd some
to carry on

Conversation miles apart. The winds
breezed up around noon and I went
below. By night time, Moon fulls then. Husband
makes out to go after a large whale
Mate's boat had dead. I am afraid to sleep—sit
think and sew. Sometime later
cutting out in my quarters, the light so weak
I catch myself dozing off
and on, get two pairs of white duck pants cut,
then stitching goosefeathers from
Cooper's Goose saved last month in a Pillow. Hear
wind think when will Jonathan wear
clothes I make tonight. How soon ago, Husband was
Right next my Elbow

possibly in eminent Danger. I
picture the Catcher struck by Shark
killer whale and Worse. I would Run for the Book
never mind my nightclothes. Pray strength,
swing heavy Lanterns and Say all I mean to save
my Beloved by a hair. Far away I hear
Commotion over the water's motion, the men holler
clamor exhausted back on board. On deck,

praise God, I do not expect waving Lanterns for
Flags or the Difficult book. The men are excited
hungry in their fatigue, all thankful. I am happy
forgetting my nightdress. I look up
misty over Flags. All on a sudden I remember. This
is called wig-wagging.

Jenny Martinson, Whaling Captain's Widow, Addresses the Historical Society

If Husband had not passed to his long long Home
he could have told you everything: the room
where Napoleon breathed his last
that had a Bust of him sitting on a monument. Fido's
persevering death. The mahomet village where the boy
crossed himself on the veranda
kneeling on a mat, putting his head to the floor
very sincere over and over. The day
Husband took himself ashore in white pants hunting
the scared traitor of a mate and come back
muddy at night, bleeding in black native dress.
The eight-year-old King in his Mother's house
who never goes out before age 18
when he can suddenly. The Sultan's 20-room House
on a hill forbidden to women, seven wives, cushions
piled high and trouble

with his feet. Husband could
always relate exact details: the sea-creature
not quite lobster, we put up in rum.
The Tahiti kanaka who fell down from aloft. His feet
slipped out from under him. He hit
head against the iron rail
doubled up like a log in water. The chicken soup
flavored with cockroach and tea
steeped in spider. When you consider the snake skin
where he shed it off and the nearly 300
horse-men on horses, it says how much whaling
improves you. On a blowy day, the men cutting in
for a greasy time everywhere on deck, you
reflect the almighty loves you. We sat in Chief's
hut on a mat drinking coconut milk
while he sent for his wives. The mat was made of
Rattan. The Hut of Bamboo. Wives

had on large hats.
Some had calico cloth put up on one shoulder
come down to the opposite hip. Some did not have
any. All the women wore calico skirts. Men had

a band round their waist
two inches wide. At one end of the hut sat a woman
making cloth. The other end was afire
where they cooked. Both were smoky. Farther on
natives rowed out to Ship with their hair
colored various colors white red black, holes in
their noses and ears with sticks
stuck through. Some had small teeth made up one way
or another. The last day we set sail
for New Grounds I stood on the Potato pen, waved my
pocket-chief till the Island was little
less than a Whale and the smoke almost a Spout.
These people do not have chimneys.

Susan Elbe

Susan Elbe is the author of *Eden in the Rearview Mirror* (Word Press) and a chapbook, *Light Made from Nothing* (Parallel Press). Her poems appear or are forthcoming in many journals and anthologies, including *Blackbird, diode, MARGIE, North American Review, Salt Hill*, and *A Fierce Brightness: Twenty-five Years of Women's Poetry* (Calyx Books). Among her awards are the inaugural Lois Cranston Memorial Poetry Prize (*Calyx*), the Council for Wisconsin Writers Lorine Niedecker Award, and fellowships to Vermont Studio Center and Virginia Center for Creative Arts. She lives in Madison, Wisconsin. www.susanelbe.com

January's Child

Finally, I wanted to give up my grief,
wanted to rid myself of the couch's bad upholstery,
the sooty pipes of the oil stoves,

too many winters.
I was tired of being northern,
gray, prickly as wool.

Those whimpers at the door were mine:
bone-beggar, orphan, stray,
the past frozen to my coat like ice.

Short afternoons when light flaked the sky
to a wafer of mica, I started looking for the sun
in my soup, in other lit windows,

ready to ride the Archer bus, anywhere
but that overheated house of long faces.
I didn't care how far I had to go,

or if I had to slog through heavy snow
deeper than the first storm.
I didn't know hard seasons keep returning.

Even in summer, everywhere I went
I found a child's scuffed tie-shoe
on the sidewalk filled with ice.

The Country of Dying

All week, the sky
slung and deeper slung, hammock
of clouds swinging down.
She wakes in a cabin to rough
walls and dusky windows
translucent as the oil stove's isinglass.

Birds call for rain
and then it rains. Late autumn,
the bare spines of trees
bend, their supple limbs bend,
their shadows lowering
and lifting like the arms of men at work.

She knows this place,
the creaky bed springs, iron
pump, tin cups reflecting all
the dear smooth surfaces. She knows
too the dark wet wind
whistling in. Sometimes it blows so hard

from such a long way,
years away, she wishes she had
shimmed the chinks, hammered in
thin wedges of dry wood
to keep out what sidles
in the corner, scratches by the wall.

She's seen better days,
a time when children spilled from her
like cherries from an apron,
when light and weather drove
her life and through her—
rain, hard sun, snow, and shimmer,

she says, *shimmer*
on the dusty floorboards, over there
inside the cupboard, outside

crinkling in the trees. A brown leaf
slaps the window like a hand.
So far inland, still she smells the sea.

Patricia Fargnoli

Patricia Fargnoli has published six collections of poetry. Her newest book, *Then, Something* (Tupelo Press, 2009) won the ForeWord Poetry Book of the Year Award Silver Award and the Shelia Mooton Book Award. She's published poems in *The Harvard Review, Green Mountains Review, Alaska Quarterly, Massachusetts Review* and *Poetry International*. A Macdowell Fellow, she was the New Hampshire Poet Laureate from 2006-2009.

Acknowledgments

"When Women Went Downtown" appears in *The Comstock Review*
"Seventy-Two, Mid-Winter" and "Over the White River" appear in *Green Mountains Review*
"Should the Fox Come Again to My Cabin in the Snow" appears in *The Alaska Quarterly*

When Women Went Downtown

The city was brick and stone in the time
before glass and steel. In those days
the city was streets of women.
They climbed down from buses
in seal skin, navy straw hats stuck with pearl drop pins,
their double-knotted Red Cross shoes,
clutching black cowhide purses, leading the children.

They lunched in tea rooms
on chicken-a-la-king and quartered sandwiches
but never wine—and never with men.
Rising in the smoky air,
their voices blended—silver striking off silver.
They haunted book rental booths,
combed aisles of threads and zippers,

climbed to the theater balconies, the palaces
where Astaire dipped and turned them
into more than they were.
In the late afternoons they crowded the winter dusk
waiting at the Isle-of-Safety, for the bus
with the right name to carry them home
to the simmer of soup on the stove,
the fire's sweet red milk.

Evenings, far over the tiny houses
the wind swept the black pines like a broom,
stars swirled in their boiling cauldron of indigo
and the children floated to sleep to the women's song
zipping the night together, to the story
of the snow goose who went farther and farther
and never returned.

Seventy-Two, Mid-Winter

In the night, then, at 3 a.m., the woman rises
to write down her dream, the dream
escaping even as she writes it,
the way her memory now seems to escape
the moment an incident is over,
as if the past has retreated into that misty world
where it hunkers forever beyond recall.

It is quiet at this hour, shades drawn,
the cat in deep sleep under the table,
his big yellow body a lesson in relaxation.
She wonders if she might learn from him. Outside,
the cold has increased, night pushes
up against the windows, only the lamp
on her desk keeps it from the room.

Yesterday, she was ill, a fleeting illness, but hard
all the same. It's left her weakened. The dream
was something about a science museum
with broken elevators and her struggling
to climb between floors. Then she's raped
on a dark mountain, and then there's a murder,
not hers, but close enough to jolt her awake.

Where is her safety now? Life for her more and more
about protection, even the words to write this down,
harder and harder to find as though they, too,
have retreated into that vast unreachable interior.
She wishes the old dream of the peacocks strolling
her walk would return, or the one about the mansion
on the hill with its fiercely glowing fireplace.

Over the White River

the hawks are turning slow spirals

time moves in all directions

and is still. I am writing a letter

to my longtime love

who lives in another geography

tied in to the prison of his body.

I am wanting to bring him back

into my life but he is lost in the past and pain.

I have been alone a long time

walking the length of my two rooms,

fifteen steps north, then south.

Rusty asleep on his cat tower.

Miles away, the river lengthens out

under the redtails riding thermals.

Though I am not there, I have seen it

in all its swirl and shining.

If it could take me to my love today

I'm not sure I'd go with it.

What power does it have

against these distances between us.

Should the Fox Come Again to My Cabin in the Snow

Then, the winter will have fallen all in white

and the hill will be rising to the north,

the night also rising and leaving,

dawn light just coming in, the fire out.

Down the hill running will come that flame

among the dancing skeletons of the ash trees.

I will leave the door open for him.

Annie Finch

Annie Finch is the author of five books of poetry, including *Eve, Calendars*, and the forthcoming *Spells: New and Selected Poems.* Her books and anthologies on poetics include *A Formal Feeling Comes, An Exaltation of Forms, The Body of Poetry*, and *A Poet's Ear.* Her work also includes a poetry CD, translation, verse plays, and creative collaboration merging poetry with music, visual art, and dance. She is Director of the Stonecoast MFA program in creative writing at the University of Southern Maine.

Acknowledgments

"Glow on the Road" appears in *Runes Magazine*
"Your Forest" appears in *National Poetry Review*

Glow on the Road

Glow on the road, and dusk's October opens
Blue against chimneys, steep eaves, stiff walls into — harbor?
Is the door open? Blue-purple, it leans inward, lilting,

Although it is shadowed, and closed. Does the roof bend a little?
Yes, into the earth, where the burgundy's surging foundation
Twists, grasps and threatens to swallow the settling floor.

Peach-softened burgundy field stretching almost too far,
waiting behind the house, not opening still;
shadows that open under the stiff, tangled eaves—

Is that a shutter? Then what is the orange behind it?
Light from the tree. Not an opening. Light from the tree.

But the house is a house; the house is as steady as silence,
And no-one can see it until they have stopped on the road—

Your Forest

Your forest goes green as love.
Your shadowing ferns ride the ground.
Moss they dapple curls above
stones your glacier trembled down.

Your night is sadness well-contained
inside the sap that runs the stem
of plants that grow along the night
and root at morning. Joy finds them.

Oceans, lost because they are vast
(like ruined roads left on the land)
take your kind waters home each time
that they, pushing raptly at the sand,

make tides with your recovered rain.
The ocean is at peace again.
Far algae grows. The blue stays smooth.
In dim light, the beach is soothed.

Your forest goes as green as love,
your night is sadness well-contained,
and oceans, lost because they are vast,
make tides with your recovered rain.

Kathleen Flenniken

Kathleen Flenniken's first book of poems, *Famous* (University of Nebraska Press, 2006), won the *Prairie Schooner* Book Prize and was named a Notable Book by the American Library Association. Her second collection, *Plume*, is an examination of the Hanford Nuclear Site and has been chosen by Linda Bierds for the *Pacific Northwest Poetry Series* (University of Washington Press, 2012). Her honors include fellowships from the NEA and Artist Trust and a 2012 Pushcart Prize.

Acknowledgments

"The State of the World" appears in *The Iowa Review*
"To Dotted Lines" appears in *The Adroit Journal*
"Fifty" appears in *Green Mountains Review* as "The Oboe Solo"

The State of the World

On a night train. Cabins dark, all the couchettes
taken, just a strobe of brown light as she prowls

for someplace to recline. She's alone, thrilled
in a fearful way, sliding down so her cheek kisses leather,

thub thub and sway. When did that man appear
in the door? She is terrified by his flickering expression.

Did I say this is wartime, that she's lost too much
that she loves? And the rivers they cross are sludge,

the fish below asleep or dead. Guards wait at the border
with guns, checking papers: it isn't hard to imagine

his mouth as an altar, that she is grateful
for buttons, for what's silky tumbled to the floor.

You would grant me this: prisoners somewhere
are meeting eyes after swimming alone in a calamity

of fear and boredom and finding corners and bunks
and passageways where they offer relief to bodies

once tethered to souls. Isn't that how they reel in
and check their lines? In the backseat of a car,

in a bathroom stall. I'm thinking all this on my side
of our beautiful restaurant meal after you describe

the mess with your clients, the too-big mortgage,
the housework impasse with your husband,

when you confess you are sleeping side by side
without touching, that you haven't made love in years.

You still love him, you insist, there's no one new—

I'm afraid to say how many times I've heard this—

it's just desire that's gone.
The life we've made is killing us and here's the proof.

To Dotted Lines

that instruct
where to
fold
paper hearts,
cut tabs
on Betsy McCall's
skirt and ice skates,
walk
from Patient Intake to
Emergency Room A.

Short cut
for your pawn
rounding the
Huckleberry Hound
game board.

Dividing
lanes
and states.
Demarking
theoretical
landings for
bank robbers
in parachutes,
hundred-year floods,
nuclear fallout.

Asymptotes
at 0 and π.
Maximum volume,
minimum height,
finish line.

The detectible
connection
between a wife

and somebody else's
man.

Warning you
in urgent Morse code—
dash, dash, dash.
Oh, oh, oh—

zones
vulnerable
to touch.
Before-
and after-
silhouettes
of love.

Trajectory
of a bullet
before
the trigger's pulled.
Outline
of a body
where it lay.

Awaiting
your signature,
scissors,
dancing feet.

Denoting
whispers,
caught breath,

ghost map
of your grave.

Fifty

This is the city at early dusk: rain suspended,
glossy streets hissing with passing cars.

In an amber-lit department store, young women
stroke blush on customers' cheeks.

A shopper lingers at a rounder of evening dresses,
stops at a headless mannequin fitted in merino wool.

She considers the sweater's deep v, feels for her throat
and surveys the islands of jewel-colored merchandise,

the glimpse of bare-limbed trees outside wrapped
in delicate white lights. When she was a little girl,

tumbleweeds blew against her bedroom window
and her mother dabbed wool wax cream on her face

to protect her from the biting wind. Now
her mother and father are gone, she is reminded

by an elevator bell, by the click of high-heeled boots
on marble. Tonight, in a velvet seat

in a burnished symphonic hall, she will listen, rapt,
to a German orchestra play Schumann.

Damn the world, damn loving it this desperately—
the oboe breaking out like a great soaring owl

as she sits dumbfounded in the dark.

Rachel Contreni Flynn

Rachel Contreni Flynn was born in Paris in 1969 and raised in a small farming town in Indiana. Her second full-length collection of poetry, *Tongue*, won the Benjamin Saltman Award and was published in 2010 by Red Hen Press. Her chapbook, *Haywire*, was published by Bright Hill Press in 2009, and her first book, *Ice, Mouth, Song*, was published in 2005 by Tupelo Press, after winning the Dorset Prize. She was awarded a Fellowship from the National Endowment for the Arts in 2007. Her work has often been nominated for Pushcart Prizes, and she received two literature grants from the Illinois Arts Council. She is an instructor in poetry at Northwestern University and a graduate of Indiana University and the Warren Wilson College MFA Program. Rachel lives in Gorham, Maine with her husband and their two children. www.rachelcontreniflynn.com

For Those In Need of Blessed Abundance

Remember French's Quarry: green water,
and deep. Mysterious warm spots

in the shadows. And the storm
that inevitably came, sent you scampering

to the ledge to rest. The world slacked—
gray quiet entire—then blazed back upon you,

sun in the face, peering at a century of rain.
Don't forget the boy, thin, but with promise,

launching from the rock, so sure of the depth
he hollered while diving. Shout gasp disappear.

Nothing bad happens here. A place
blasted empty then filled with nothing

that harms us. Warmth and storm, the release
of a young body into forgiving air. Going home,

the sacks of chips, grape sodas, the boy
with his skinny arm lightly upon you.

Chime

The children smashed
the mother's glass doll
and could never

fix it. They held the bits

and cut themselves
trying.

The mother cried, then
was silent.

After the breaking the world
became surprising:

winter brought steam,
summer, ice. One morning
the mother seemed done

with the punishment.

She grabbed lengths of piano wire
and a short stick

and rigged a curtain
of ragged glass.

It hung

on the porch
and made rough songs
the children learned

to bear
in all their comings
and goings

and in sleep.

Stubble

I've come with my straight razors, done
with this town, done with the sad brown

microphones, cattails I'll level at last
and be released. My dad has sold the house

in which I was saddened. Sold away the brace
of raspberries, the peeling sheds,

the deep thorny trees, all my hiding places.
Even the basement—that's bought too,

the air there cold with bluestones,
sharp with the taste of ash and salt.

I've come back not to weep
but to cut down. First in wide arcs,

then tenderly, delicately, as I will when my dad
is very old, and I hold a basin under his chin

to scrape away whiskers in whiteness.
I must be finished telling my story

to the ditches and ponds, except to say
you've been very kind. And forgive me.

Forgive me all my sharpness,
my sadness here.

Bring It

I've been waiting
to understand
the flaw for which

I am responsible.

To stand under.
To be humbled.

The night Grace
and I go owling
is the coldest

of the year, the moon
so sharp the sky
seems in pain.

I piggy-back her
across the pasture,
into the woods

until under
an ash tree we see
a tiny hoot owl

not hooting.

My daughter
is warm in the dark
and loves me.

It could be this easy.
I could just shut up.

What she needs
tonight is hot cocoa
and a mother

who brings it.
We head for home,

and I do.

Rebecca Foust

Rebecca Foust received her MFA in Creative Writing from Warren Wilson College in January 2010. Her books include *God, Seed: Poetry and Art About the Natural World* (Tebot Bach Press 2010), *All That Gorgeous, Pitiless Song*, awarded the Many Mountains Moving Prize and published in 2010, and *Mom's Canoe* and *Dark Card* awarded the Robert Phillips Chapbook Prizes in consecutive years and published by Texas Review Press in 2008 and 2009. Recent poems appear in *Arts & Letters Journal, The Hudson Review, Margie, North American Review, Poetry Daily*, and elsewhere. www.rebeccafoust.com

Flame

for Fatima Omar Mahmud al-Najar, Palestinian Martyr

Not the change but another
kind of pause: the body

in paraphrase, working loose
like a tooth, hair releasing

in drifts like dead leaves
in late fall.

They took it all, leaving her
unable to eat

more than a mote. She was
burnt trunk and root.

But they forgot that what fire
eats it also ignites,

and so great a heat will anneal
sand and salt

into glass seamed with healed
fractures, a dense lump

of dumb quartz struck, flaked
again and again

to hone the ritual blade, rage
finally refined

into the clarity of pure air,
its precise blessing

folded and wrapped about
her slim waist, released

finally as one thin flame,
rising.

Mandate

She quit, and went home to tend her husband,
children and garden.

Stun of relief, the simple equation of add food
to hunger, and a voice

will stop crying. But her husband, it turned out
didn't want tending,

and the children grew up. She dressed and undressed
the border beds, pressing her face

to the soft, pink cheeks of impatiens. She drove
to the grocery store

three times in one day, her cupboards still
so bare. She walked

to the jetty in winter, watched the sea shift
in ebb and eddy, fail to congeal

into a shape she could recognize. Until
the day the waves seized, stood

still, and gave back reflection: the city hall
jail, its common cell sink

ringing with milk wrung from the breast
of a woman who looked

straight back at her. She gazed into time's
quartz heart, stared down

the years. The stars leaned in, as useful
in navigation and augur

as they'd ever been, above a sea frozen
in cataract, glittering ice-clear.

Suzanne Frischkorn

Suzanne Frischkorn is the author of *Girl On A Bridge* (2010), and *Lit Windowpane* (2008) both from Main Street Rag Publishing. In addition she is the author of five chapbooks, most recently *American Flamingo* (2008). Her poems have appeared in *Barn Owl Review, Copper Nickel, Ecotone, Indiana Review, North American Review, Verse Daily, Conversation Pieces: Poems That Talk to Other Poems*, part of the *Everyman's Library Pocket Series*, (Knopf) and elsewhere. Her honors include the Aldrich Poetry Award for her chapbook *Spring Tide*, selected by Mary Oliver, and an Artist Fellowship from the Connecticut Commission on Culture & Tourism.

A Poem Found in the Foyer

It was really hot we had left

        the front door open,

the screen door was shut,

        but not locked

and they walked in,

        right up the steps into our foyer

        to bang on the interior

        French door. I scurried

to the door to see

and there they were—

        The Mormons.

Two young men in short-sleeve button downs and skinny black ties,

with bad haircuts.

They introduced themselves

        as Elders, asked if they could

educate me

as part of their two-year mission.

I didn't want

                to invite them in—

I started

                thinking about female

Mormons—where they fit

into the whole damn scheme

and the Elder doing the talking

must have sensed

he was losing me—

he shook

my hand and gave me a card

with a website

that could educate me,

but first

he wrote down his phone number

just in case I wanted to call him

and have him

educate me personally.

Guess I still got it.

My Body as an Urban Landscape

My body's lexicon is like the clamor of flocks,

or the swarm of bees

under a crawlspace,

it's a swathe of

ornamental grass. It's the heft,

the angle, the swell,

a balm.

My body's

lexicon emits

constellations—

limestone
and thorn, flare and douse,

haunch and dodge.

The wind aligns

gems in its basin.

First Thaw

Last autumn I left the seed heads on the black-eyed Susans,

now they are an etching against snow

a small consolation for birds.

January ends tomorrow.

Overcome by sun, sand and salt this winter's ice

begins its slow melt.

The garden seems like a dream at the edge of consciousness,

difficult to recall.

Perennials returned to earth—yarrow, dianthus, myrtle.

The tulips and lilies asleep.

This morning the birds natter outside my window.

What's there to say?

I want to ask them, unable to wake from a weeklong

stupor, unable to move without a great force of will.

I pull back the sheers and see bright blue sky,

soft cumulus clouds,

the ocean in my front yard.

Half-Light

The first bright sun of the year and I am unable to face it.

Sunlight glitters in gutter streams and thins snow banks

just enough to reveal their entrails—

decayed leaves, blackened branches. By afternoon the sun

is unable to break through the clouds. As we leave

to pick up my son my daughter catches snowflakes on her tongue.

In the backyard a woodpecker coaxes a beetle out of the pine bark.

Sometimes no amount of burrowing will suffice.

February, the month where giving in to dormancy

is most seductive, it feels farthest from spring.

I remind myself the earthworms are busy aerating the soil,

and that dormancy is a form of conservation. I remind myself

to pick up my son, to go to the bank, the post office, the market.

These small trips, daily and ordinary,

get me through the longest month.

The afternoon's hush, interrupted by snowplow

and small children running through the house, fills in the night.

I wake before dawn to find our neighborhood

buffed in silence, its hard edges softened.

With sunrise comes the rhythmic scrape of shovels against pavement.

The snow appears brighter in the half-light.

The wind tosses up sparkling motes.

Jeannine Hall Gailey

Jeannine Hall Gailey is the author of *Becoming the Villainess* (Steel Toe Books) and *She Returns to the Floating World* (Kitsune Books.) Her work has been featured on NPR's *The Writer's Almanac, Verse Daily*, and in the *Year's Best Fantasy and Horror*. She volunteers as an editorial consultant for *Crab Creek Review* and currently teaches at the MFA program at National University.
www.webbish6.com

Acknowledgments

"Uzurazuki," "Advice Given Before My Wedding," and "In the Month of Quail" appear in *She Returns to the Floating World* (Kitsune Books, 2011)

Uzurazuki (The Month of Quail)

Wednesday I tried to lie down but couldn't sleep. Outside it was daylight, I had forgotten my name and who I was. A quail kept calling, one quail all alone, outside my window. Was he waiting for me? I knew what day of the week it was, what outfit I was wearing, but memory is like that sometimes, water, it slips through. A quail crying alone for six days. I wish I knew where we were going, this quail and I. Whether I was going to leap through the window into some other life. Whether or not I would wake up one day and suddenly know flight. Follow the clouds away from here. Follow some dream I can't remember. What did you say?

The name of the rocks here,
not granite, not limestone. Something
more blue. Agate?

The way you said my name sounded like wings. Maybe I do have wings. What to remember, the way I made that sound that sounded like crying, the taste of rust rising in my throat like wings.

In the Month of Quail

The shoes I am wearing bruise the top of my feet. On our trail there are rabbits and waxwings, a heron in the stream, exotic loud swans. Stomping through the grass I discover my quail, now he's become six—the father and mother, four crownless children. Why had he been calling at my window? Was he calling for her, his mate, his children? Isolated from family, solitary, a state foreign to quail? Quail stand for togetherness in dreams, because, as you see, they hoot to each other, they shake together as one covey, they wander up through the thicket, calling out in the blackberries.

He stands guard,
proudly. They are round
like little fall fruits.

Where will these quail lead me? Already the dusk is following, the swallows are becoming bats in the August darkness. Beware of sitting alone in your little house, he tells me from the thorny branches, beware of listening too long to the calls of tear-shaped birds, using them for guidance.

Advice Given to Me Before My Wedding

Better to be the lover than the beloved, you'll have passion.
Better to be the beloved, a sure thing, a lifetime of that.

He is more beautiful but you,
you have more power. Which is to say,

you are just like your brother. Lift your eyes
and people do what you say. Who knows why.

Men are like breakfast cereal. You have to pick one.
Fish in the sea, a dime a dozen. They are singing for you, now.

Keep your own bank account. Keep working.
Give him a blowjob, and he'll volunteer to take out the trash.

You are mine, says the beloved, and I am yours.
Whither you go I will go. Honey and milk are under her tongue.

Cancer and Taurus, very compatible.
You're the hard-charger, he's the homemaker.

Don't stop wearing lipstick. Don't put on any weight.
Don't buy the dress too soon. If you go on the pill, your breasts will swell.

One day you might regret. You might do better.
You could do worse. One man's as good as another.

Wear my old pearls. Here's the blue, a handkerchief embroidered with tears.
If you won't wear heels, you'll look short in the pictures.

If you don't wear a veil, people will say you're not a virgin.
Good luck, glad tidings, a teddy, a toaster. So long, farewell.

Maya Ganesan

Maya Ganesan is a thirteen-year-old poet from Redmond, Washington, who began writing poetry at the age of four. Her first collection of poetry, *Apologies to an Apple*, was published by Classic Day Publishing in early 2009. She can be found online at www.mayaganesan.com and www.mayaganesan.blogspot.com

Negative Four Hundred

The rain carves patterns
into my window.

It will be different this time,
I promise,
the words crisscross over
stones.

I remember she told me,
Curved hips,
they are like waves.

She could hear my heartbeats,
every breath.

Every day we mapped it,
found a beginning but no end.

I whisper the name
of my being:
human.

Undefined

Warm shades of orange
flicker, reaching for the sky.

Inside her pocket,
she keeps receipts,
long lists of numbers,
folded charts.

She brushes quiet
out of her dark hair,
finds silver
in a stretch of black.

It is October.

She mails a letter
to nobody—
where will it go?

I ask
for a basket of tears.
When

will the fire burn her palms?

She listens
for the sharp staccato
of endless voices.

Time and speed,
undefined.

Arielle Greenberg

Arielle Greenberg is the co-author, with Rachel Zucker, of *Home/Birth: A Poemic* (1913 Press), and author *of My Kafka Century* (Action Books), *Given* (Verse/Wave) and the chapbooks *Shake Her* and *Farther Down: Songs from the Allergy Trials*. She is co-editor of three anthologies: with Rachel Zucker, *Starting Today: 100 Poems for Obama's First 100 Days* (Iowa) and *Women Poets on Mentorship: Efforts and Affections* (Iowa); and with Lara Glenum, *Gurlesque* (Saturnalia). Twice featured in *Best American Poetry* and the recipient of a MacDowell Colony fellowship, she is the founder-moderator of the poet-moms listserv and teaches at Columbia College Chicago. www.ariellegreenberg.net

On Bodily Love

Used to be is a long way off,
a white-shoed parade of funkadelic horns
making circles in the air in procession:
how our bodies took notice one of the other,
and comfort, and something more sinister and delicious as well.

My nostalgia for it is the same as for the grain
of a Seventies Polaroid, everyone orange-
haired, blasted, birthday caked.
The date stamped on the edge
to show you can't get it back.

Now we both just eat up our girl,
the one we made together in our bed,
eat and eat her,
flesh-and-limb love, mouthy love.
From the other room right now I listen to her
lie under your kisses and your hands and laugh,
a little crazed, basking.

Does it make me sad? Do I miss it?
It's more like a song I'm glad to hear again,
almost forgot I liked as much as I do.

In Cheryl's Novel

In the novel—which is based on life—the dying mother calls her children home.
And home they come,
though home it's hardly to them half-grown,
and they push like animals at meat until they know the reason for the call
and then in all they gather, like at a fire circle.

What you do instead of this:
I'd call it flinging out.
Flinging out our things in duffel bags onto the sidewalk,
flinging out the old rose gold watches we were meant to have,
flinging out the books you bought for my baby just so she can't have them.
We may be animals in dark burglar masks,
twice the size of any decent daughters but oh
you can't say we didn't try to stay right by the wild fire.
Though this is what you say, and turn the flames up higher.

There's no fucking sense to it.
I have a daughter too, and I miss her while she's sleeping.
I mean, I sleep terribly with my girl sweated to my body, in my bed
and yet I want her in my bed. In my mouth, my skin. Even closer.
Every second edible in its sweetness and its goneness.
This must be what it means to live for someone.

So I don't know. Did you never feel this in your fur,
the slap of a love so hot it can only mean mother?
I would like to say one day that I miss you
but right now there is no bed far enough away.
In Cheryl's novel it doesn't turn out this way.

Kate Greenstreet

Kate Greenstreet is the author of *The Last 4 Things* and *case sensitive* (both from Ahsahta Press) and five chapbooks, most recently *CALLED* (Delete Press, 2011). Her work can be found in *Chicago Review, Boston Review, Fence, Volt,* and other journals. www.kickingwind.com

Acknowledgments

"If water covers the road" appears in *case sensitive* (Ahsahta Press, 2006)
"Leaving the Old Neighborhood" appears in *Learning the Language* (Etherdome Press, 2005)

Leaving the Old Neighborhood

In the dream I slept all night and you were a saint,
your shirt stained yellow near the heart, spontaneously, blue under the arms.

It turns out to be music, our prayers. We went out to tell our mother
in her bulb-lit grotto.
Chipping
a little, but she still looks great,
her arms outstretched and her veil,
refuge of sinners, cause
of our joy.

Wisdom had built herself a house in the dream, I was twins,
I was looking for something.

How can the poet be called unlucky
who rides on the back of the colt?

If water covers the road

It's something about living on a former
airforce base in winter
in the desert, after they've all gone.

You can't help thinking of them during the days.
Going out or coming back,
waiting. The soldiers.

They're everywhere, and mostly
I don't know their names.

I asked a man in the hardware store for help.
"The only thing you want
to remember," he said,
"about the dead

is that the bottom
of everything is theirs.
The bottom of the river, the bottom of
every drawer.
If water should cover the road,
the bottom of that puddle belongs to them."

We're in the midst of letting go.
Knot by knot,
finger by finger.

Becoming one
of the three or four people
we might have been.

You can't always walk away.

"You can think about it," he said, "but
don't believe in it: on the earth
already means under the sky."

Lola Haskins

Lola Haskins' tenth collection of poetry, *The Grace to Leave* is forthcoming from Anhinga Press. Her ninth, *Still, the Mountain*, appeared in 2010. Among her earlier works are *Solutions Beginning with A* (illustrated fables), *The Rim Benders, Desire Lines: New and Selected Poem, Extranjera*, and *Forty-Four Ambitions for the Piano*. Ms. Haskins' prose work includes a poetry advice book and a nonfiction book about fifteen Florida Cemeteries (forthcoming from the University Press of Florida). www.lolahaskins.com

Acknowledgments

"El Amor y la Mujer" appears in *The Atlantic* (the English version); the translation is the poet's and is unpublished
"The Interpreters" and "In Tide Pools" appear in *Hudson Review*

The Interpreters

Only those shallow as creeks in drought misunderstand
our helplessness before landscapes that reach the throat.
The rest of us know that cliffs or clouds can be addressed
only on their own terms, and in languages that have nothing
to do with words. There's a school for this, in a country
which is a long train ride off, and from birth some of us
have aspired to study there. But when our applications are
returned with blank pages inside, we don't know what to do.

So we watch for signs—the tone-marks of a hawk's angled
wings before she drops to grass—the directions a dying wave
has fingered onto the sand. We would have despaired long ago
were it not that once in awhile, one of our tongue-tied number
vanishes. And returns glorious—fluent in storm cloud, sage,
or boiling lava. A child's aptitude for language may surface
early, as when his mother notices smoke skirling from his mouth
as she points at the sky, or red rock appearing in his hands
when she says canyon. Wanting to keep him close, she may
not tell him about the train. It will not matter. He will find it.

Perhaps there are teachers among us. There's a man I've
been following for hours, who walks the narrow trail as if
he had no feet. I think by that, and by the way his hair
brightens at the base of his neck, he may know. I quicken
my pace, to see if it was he singing overhead, but he
must have been speaking sky, because when I turn
the corner, a cloud is rising off the stones, rimmed
with an eloquence I have encountered only in dreams.

In Tide Pools

Lavender-spined urchins reside. And anemones with
wavy mouths. And periwinkle snails, full of themselves
because they have been given such a beautiful name.
And over these low-dwellers, fine-haired grasses drift,
as if underwater there were always a wind. And since
these communities, not touching, are like language
groups that have grown apart, it is not surprising that
each has its legends. In one, it is said that the Maker,
taking pity on the rocks' empty cups, filled them. In
this way, the rocks, once beggars, became kings. In
another, that certain stars, unhappy to be among
multitudes, found solace in these smaller skies.
Elsewhere, it is said that long ago the dwellers in these
valleys lived deep. But slowly and slowly, waverush
drew them upward. And now they are visited every
day by her who, breaking over them, leaves parts of
herself, which they drink and want for nothing. It is
not only humans who have religion. On the edge of
the sea, the finger limpets see the Almighty, and cling.

Love

She tries it on, like a dress.
She decides it doesn't fit
and starts to take it off.
Her skin comes, too.

~

El Amor y la Mujer

Se lo prueba, como si fuera un vestido.
Decide que no le queda
y empieza a quitárselo.
Su piel se desprende, tambien.

Eloise Klein Healy

Eloise Klein Healy, Distinguished Professor of Creative Writing Emerita, was the founding chair of the MFA in Creative Writing Program at Antioch University Los Angeles. She is the author of six books of poetry, most recently *The Islands Project: Poems For Sappho*. Healy directed the Women's Studies Program at California State University Northridge and taught in the Feminist Studio Workshop at The Woman's Building in Los Angeles. Arktoi Books is her imprint with Red Hen Press.

Acknowledgments

"Love Poem From Afar," "Hardscape," and "Flower Shop" appear in *The Islands Project: Poems For Sappho* (Red Hen Press, 2007)

Love Poem From Afar
for Colleen

I

This morning I'm more lonely than the sky,
that flattened tray of tin and rain

before the robin's quick array of ruddy breasts
displayed the air a way that's new

as when in their noisy gang
they flew against the blue

like stitches in a quilt
that's being aired out with a shake.

I take some solace watching starlings
with their yellow bills root among the leaves.

They're plump with some success, those clerks.
Field notes, perhaps, or a survey of the seeds.

II

Your day still sits under the horizon
while mine unfolds in steps I take
to make myself familiar here:
breakfast in the kitchen, carry tea upstairs,
watch a squirrel hop across the lawn,
keep a careful list of birds I've seen.
Tai chi, before or after.

I know we're on the same planet,
the same sun coming in the east window.
I know how and why time zones float
like gauzy curtains across the globe.
But here's the fact that sends me to the page.

I want to see you every day we're in this life,
mark change with you as we change, as we age,
for it's true, as you say, it took a long time

for us to find each other and much pain.
I think only of telling you
about these birds, these swales of rain
and flowering trees so different from our own.

This would be another world
with you in it.

No—you are the world.

Hardscape

Say it's the memory of early mornings
in the shop, the power lift raising a car
in the dawn light, steam lifting off the highway
in front of the garage, and tools
coming to life at the touch of a hand.

Say it's the clang of things, the ping
of ball bearings pouring into a pan
and then a gush of gas from the pump,
the cleaning rag running over
the steely marbles to spark their shine.

Up the hill, the farm horse's shoes
tap against the gravel on the road,
the tack clinks and groans, the barn doors
bang and creak and corn stalks screech
against each other in the wind.

Say it made me hanker for hard things,
want to get outdoors first light, handle sticks
and dead tires, bang old mufflers together
and bam a ball peen hammer
against a scrap of sheet metal behind the shop.

It made me not want dolls and the demands
of indoors—quiet in the parlor, quiet by the stove.
It made me a woman of landscape and weather
and suspicious of my place. Say it gave me
a chrome handle to a different and difficult world.

Flower Shop

Stepping in from the street,
the heat would drop away
and a sigh of greenery
announce itself.

First it was "Bill's Flowers" lettered in blue
on the window and the white panel truck.
Bill was a blond model-type,
something short of 6 feet tall
and skinny in a tight jeans kind of way.

And then he was gone. Men were dying
overnight, it seemed, from some new death blow
eventually named AIDS. Did Bill ever look sick?
Who knew what to look for,
we were just shopping for flowers.

It was a place to order up a special bouquet,
pink *Heliconia* or white ginger blossoms, maybe.
Thai orchards with sweet baby faces,
pricey but spectacular. Always something
exotic highlighting the beautiful window displays.

Paul took over after Bill died. The truck got repainted
with a little pinstripe below the name "Paul's Plants".
I was buying more vases and single stems of things.
I liked to wander from room to room,
the best part of shopping there,
moving through the flower shop's damp and tactile air.

Now Paul is dead, too—his meds never worked.
The truck reads "Green & Co."
Letters in a ceramic lime,
and right at the end of the line,
two little daisies punctuating it.

I don't know Green yet. Maybe he's a survivor.
Maybe he's young. He's pretty great, though,

with the window displays. My friend Maria
thinks he has a background in set design.
All of the workers have stayed on and so has
a chill in that beautiful glade of rooms.

Jane Hirshfield

Jane Hirshfield's seventh collection of poetry, *Come, Thief,* appears from Knopf in 2011. Her other books include *After* (HarperCollins, 2006), named a best book of 2006 by *The Washington Post* and England's Financial Times, and *Given Sugar, Given Salt* (HarperCollins, 2001), a finalist for the National Book Critics Circle Award. Honors include fellowships from the Guggenheim and Rockefeller foundations, the NEA, and The Academy of American Poets, as well as five selections in *The Best American Poetry*. Hirshfield lives in the San Francisco Bay Area and reads her work widely in the U.S. and abroad.

Acknowledgments

"French Horn" appears in *The New Yorker*
"A Thought" appears in *Poetry London*
"Critique of Pure Reason" appears in *Ploughshares Magazine* and *The Best American Poetry 2007*
"Perishable, It Said" appears in *Poetry*

All of the poems above will also appear in *Come, Thief* (Knopf, 2011)

Perishable, It Said

Perishable, it said on the plastic container,
and below, in different ink,
the date to be used by, the last teaspoon consumed.

I found myself looking:
now at the back of each hand,
now inside the knees,
now turning over each foot to look at the sole.

Then at the leaves of the young tomato plants,
then at the arguing jays.

Under the wooden table and lifted stones, looking.
Coffee cups, olives, cheeses,
hunger, sorrow, fears—
these too would certainly vanish, without knowing when.

How suddenly then
the strange happiness took me,
like a man with strong hands and strong mouth,
inside that hour with its perishing perfumes and clashings.

A Thought

Some thoughts
throw off
a backward heat
as walls might,
at night, in summer.

It could happen
this moment—

Some movement.

One word's almost
imperceptible shiver.

And what was
long cold
in your left palm,
long cold in your right palm,
might find itself
malleable, warmer.

An apricot
could be planted,
in such a corner.

Critique of Pure Reason

"Like one man milking a billy-goat,
another holding a sieve beneath it,"
Kant wrote, quoting an unnamed ancient.
It takes a moment to notice the sieve doesn't matter.
In her nineties, a woman begins to sleepwalk.
One morning finding pudding and a washed pot,
another the opened drawers of her late husband's dresser.
After a while, anything becomes familiar,
though the Yiddish jokes of Auschwitz
stumbled and failed outside the barbed wire.
Perimeter is not meaning, but it changes meaning,
as wit increases distance and compassion erodes it.
Let reason flow like water around a stone, the stone remains.
A dog catching a tennis ball lobbed into darkness
holds her breath silent, to keep the descent in her ears.
The goat stands patient for two millennia,
watching without judgment from behind his strange eyes.

French Horn

For a few days only,
the plum tree outside the window
shoulders perfection.
No matter the plums will be small,
eaten only by squirrels and jays.
I feast on the one thing, they on another,
the shoaling bees on a third.
What in this unpleated world isn't someone's seduction?
The boy playing his intricate horn in Mahler's Fifth,
in the gaps between playing,
turns it and turns it, dismantles a section,
shakes from it the condensation
of human passage. He is perhaps twenty.
Later he takes his four bows, his face deepening red,
while a girl holds a viola's spruce wood and maple
in one half-opened hand and looks at him hard.
Let others clap.
These two, their ears still ringing, hear nothing.
Not the shouts of *bravo, bravo,*
not the timpanic clamor inside their bodies.
As the plum's blossoms do not hear the bee
nor taste themselves turned into storable honey
by that sumptuous disturbance.

Erin Coughlin Hollowell

Erin Coughlin Hollowell lives in Homer, Alaska, a small fishing town at the end of the road. She is originally from upstate New York and has a Bachelor of Arts degree from Cornell University, concentration writing. In 2009, she received her MFA in writing poetry from the Rainier Writing Workshop at Pacific Lutheran University. Her work has most recently been published in *Weber Studies, Alaska Quarterly Review, Terrain.org, Crab Creek Review*, and *Blue Earth Review*. She writes about poetry and writing at www.beingpoetry.net

Parts of Speech

The cloud speaks all in sibilance
to the moon. To the mountain,

it clanks together consonants
like old cowbells. All day

I have tried to hold still
long enough to listen.

There is a story
in the way my skin unfurls

when I've locked away industry.
It has some of the same words

that the cloud has, but without
direction—I've discarded verbs.

Alder columbine stone moss.
Fingertip thigh nape lip.

Purity Pie Tin

Work knobbed knuckles, willow beautiful,
smoothing pie crust with a quarry weight

into a tin rayed with knife cuts.
Television in the front room footballing

and him grunting in a barcalounger,
while she bumble-bee throats her way

through an old Hank Williams tune.
Berries from the back fence line,

wasp-ripe, plucked in morning,
waiting in a white bowl sheltered

by a linen 1943 calendar dishtowel.
Wedding band worn thin, snapped

in half and she just laughed.
Sleeps in her own bed, her sheets

lavendered, his cold feet two rooms
away. Every story a doppelganger

of her anger and his grey hat hanging
in a hotel room. Red sweet scent

teases as she scoops ice cream
into a blue dish beside a perfect slice.

He eats his in front of the game,
while she rocks on the porch. Nothing

lasts, especially not summer.

Broken

You love your dead brother
like you love the broken umbrella
hidden in the back of the hall closet.

You love the bent-back ribs
and the sad black flap of ruin,
the perfect uselessness you can't

possibly discard. Once or twice
each season, you pull it out
and wrap it in excuses, wipe

away the dust. The afternoon
light makes of it a saint's relic.
For who could not admire

the wreckage made by the wind
and the sudden astonishment
of autumn's cold rain.

Memorial

The shadows of the dead
cast themselves
on the shoulders of the road.
We go to them with empty hands,
our throats cages of language.

If they long to linger
it is not evident in their momentum;
they continue past these houses of trial and salt.

Everything gets torn away
when we learn the difference
between prayer and importuning.

Beneath the wings of birds there is a map
to where the table is set in our honor.

We are hungry but only realize it
after the wind hollows us
for the second time.
The dead pour a glass of rainwater
for a blessing.

Anna Maria Hong

Anna Maria Hong is the 2010-11 Bunting Fellow in Poetry at the Radcliffe Institute for Advanced Study. Her poems have been published or are forthcoming in journals including *New Orleans Review, Exquisite Corpse, The Journal, jubilat, Fence, Sonora Review, St. Petersburg Review, Fairy Tale Review, Mobile City, Gargoyle*, and *POOL*. Her nonfiction appears in publications such as *American Book Review, Poets & Writers*, poetryfoundation.org, *The Stranger*, and *The International Examiner*. She has received residencies from Yaddo and Djerassi and has taught creative writing at the University of Washington and UCLA Extension's Writers' Program. She is currently a Lecturer at Eastern Michigan University.

Acknowledgments

"I/Device" and "V/Departure" appear in *No Tell Motel*

from ***Medea Cycle***

I/Device

I'll tell you plainly my dear that my heart
broke like a berg when the news hit me,
and I know that word makes you stop short.
So strange, after all, to see just the tip.

They say the shadow self trails us
for fathoms like a dirty tail. Ignore
my mixed comparisons. I'm not my best.
Yesterday, you had me still. From now, we

will not exist. That will be odd, but so was
happiness. I know it's destiny,
the way I know the Argo is a blessed

ship. It's just a fact and just fantastic,
the way my whole life has been. The power.
The magic. And now the metaphors stop.

V/Departure

Whale-road. The path to Athens glittered
with blues, and as we rolled, I dove under
with those broad, gray backs through each wave. What mattered
now? A clutch of minnow breaking surface asunder,

the sun on my face burning like potential,
salt in my hair, my skin. The knowledge of you
unable to locate the source of denial.
The world billowing below this normal vessel.

The spray and scent and speed. A strafe of white
gulls peeling over the hull's wall, blooming like
bare streaks. A hint of fire on the horizon . . .

Upon leaving the kingdom where every hero's
a victim and vice versa: the V-shaped flight
of something rising in rows and rows and rows.

Holly Hughes

Holly Hughes' poems have been nominated for an *Arts and Letters* and Pushcart prize and have appeared in the *Alaska Quarterly Review* and the *Bellingham Review*, among others, as well as in several anthologies, including *Dancing With Joy: 99 Poems*. Her chapbook *Boxing the Compass* won the Floating Bridge chapbook contest in 2007. She is the editor of *Beyond Forgetting: Poems and Prose about Alzheimer's Disease* (Kent State University Press). She spends her winters teaching writing at Edmonds Community College where she co-directs the Convergence Writers Series and the Sustainability Initiative and her summers skippering and working on boats as a naturalist in Alaska. She lives in a log cabin built in the 1930s in Indianola.

On Approaching 52

She realizes she'll never be a lion tamer, tall hat and curling whip,
lions and tigers padding in circles on huge, silent paws,

that she's too late for Jacques Cousteau, balanced on the edge
of the boat, strapped into steel lungs, tilting back into the sea,

that she won't become a wildlife photographer, packing
cameras in the Himalayas in search of the snow leopard,

that even though her mother said *You can be anything you want, dear*—
at some point the trajectory that leads up begins to arc

down, that each day we learn again to live with our choices,
not knowing exactly what that meant before this.

Still, she dreams of Barnum & Bailey pulling into town at midnight,
rasp and *skreetch* of cage doors yawning wide to let out the big cats,

earth shaking as the elephants, freed, stomp down Main Street.

Finding Your Socks

Eight years after you're gone,
I find a pair, your name ironed on
in capitals—COLLEEN HUGHES—
from your months in assisted living,
where everyone's clothes ended up
in everyone else's drawers, name tags
the only way to sort out
what could still be sorted.

The tags pucker where they stick
to black & white cotton, and I slip
them on my feet, glad to carry you
with me today as you once carried
me, remembering the name tags
you sewed by hand on all my clothes
—before iron-ons—
so I could take them to camp.

Oh, the pride in seeing my name
on all my clothes—big enough
at last to go to camp alone.
How could I know those
name tags that sent you
on alone would someday
bring you back to me,
mother, lost and found.

Ann Batchelor Hursey

Ann Batchelor Hursey's work has appeared in the *Seattle Review, Crab Creek Review, Chrysanthemum*, and *Pontoon*, among others. Her poem "Wetland," is the official Shel Sheb Estuary poem. Besides collaborative work with Contemporary Quilt Artist, Priscilla Peterson, and book artist, Lou Cabeen, she has worked with composer, Paul Lewis, and written poems to compost and community gardens (Seattle P-Patch poet). Ann has been awarded writing residencies at Soapstone (Oregon) and Hypatia-in-the-Woods (Shelton, WA.) Born in Ohio, she now calls Washington State home.

Acknowledgments

"Tourist in the Season of Light" appears in *Crab Creek Review*

Tourist in the Season of Light

Thirty-thousand feet above earth, roads twist like larvae
into soil. Snow sticking to every Colorado crease;
            lakes puddle brown beneath Texan skies.

Farther east, sun slides through a chandelier of Tampa
clouds waiting for tomorrow's storm. I swear, never
            has a flight landed quite so noiselessly.

Shuttle doors advance another twenty travelers
into airport shops adorned with pastel shaded palms,
            Key Lime pies and alligator tongues.

We scatter in the wake of children's choirs
singing: *one lit candle burning*, while luggage
            rolls toward other gates. We carry on

to jobs and homes, secured by x-rays candling
an image of a gun or perhaps a spiral notebook
            too close to a tin of mints—

Made by Hand

My thumb loops yarn, inserts
the needle's tip,
pulls yarn through each stitch: right
to left, back
to front—worked-in, slipped-off
my needle—
I purse my lips and knit
this prayer shawl
to warm a friend's shoulders.
My son appears
to say, *Knitting makes you*
look older.
Startled, I think: Is this
the first time
he's seen gray on my temples?
Is it the way
I squint beneath the lamp?
My needles slide,
knit three, purl three—and then
reverse the row
below; a three beat, seed
stitch, trinity
of healing thoughts. As fingers
move I tell
him how *I cast sixty stitches,*
like my age—
My needles slide, knit three, purl
three—three beat
trinity of healing thoughts—
Me, thinking when
was the first time I thought
my parents *old?*
Unobserved, I used to watch them
sitting, side by side—
their eyes on strangers—and me
wondering when
did they put on weight, when
did their shoulders
soften? My son speaks again,
would I listen

to a Haydn solo, the piece he
needs to learn
next week? He leans against
my knees, catches
the shawl, now falling off
my lap. My
hands graze past his unkempt hair
as we listen to
this floating melody, this
slow concerto.
It's then I start my final row,
turn all that
length now gathered on the floor—
Consider skills
of binding-off. Remembering
do it loosely.

Luisa A. Igloria

Luisa A. Igloria is the author of *Juan Luna's Revolver* (2009 Ernest Sandeen Prize, University of Notre Dame), *Trill & Mordent* (WordTech Editions, 2005), and eight other books. Luisa has degrees from the University of the Philippines, Ateneo de Manila University, and the University of Illinois at Chicago, where she was a Fulbright Fellow from 1992-1995. She teaches on the faculty of Old Dominion University, where she directs the MFA Creative Writing Program. She keeps her radar tuned for cool lizard sightings. Since November 20, 2010, Luisa has been writing a poem a day at Dave Bonta's *Via Negativa* website. Luisa's author website is www.luisaigloria.com and she blogs at: www.blipfoto.com/lizardmeanders

Acknowledgments

These poems appeared previously on the *Via Negativa* website www.vianegativa.us of poet, editor and publisher Dave Bonta, as part of the "Morning Porch Poems by Luisa Igloria" series:
"Consonance" 15 January 2011
"Forager" 17 January 2011
"Speaking of__" 31 December 2010
"Despedida de Soltera" 4 January 2011

Forager

Icicles at sunrise: no even-toed ungulates
come plodding to the cherry, therefore.
But a titmouse lands there, the peachy-
brown streak in her breast the same rust
in a tree sparrow's cap or a broomsedge stem.
Some days are copper-lined, are meat and wine
and crackling logs the little match girl strikes
flint after flint to enter. I'd take her hand
and sit her on our laps, wrap her in a tufted
comforter. Small songbird, acrobatic forager,
you've buried your hoard of morsels so long
in the ground—pine and beech, oak, fruit
of the candleberry. My desire is also quietly
eager for spring. Nothing much yet on the ground—
but pry open the secrets in each gravelly seed;
carry them aloft, bear some to the one I love.

Despedida de Soltera

Three of my four music teachers were nuns. And the neighborhood referred to my very first piano teacher as the spinster—she wore dark clothing, sensible shoes, *agua de colonia flor de naranja*. She lived alone, with only part-time help; she never told anyone where she went in summer: *Soltera*. But I've always preferred this nod to solitude, to single-tude; the way impudent "l" pushes away from gossipy "o" and fakely coy "e" to bump up against "t" as if to say—So what? Years later, I'm still amazed at how much they knew: the libraries of trills and crescendos hidden underneath wimples and lace shawls; the ways they coaxed feeling from generations of wooden pupils surreptitiously kicking their legs into the piano's soundboard. Listen to the advance of notes in this passage, they'd say: surf shirring the sand, or horses' hooves soon coming around the bend. And then the clearing drenched in the scent of violets, which moves you inexplicably to tears. From my bedroom window, the chair backs in the garden are scrolled like treble clefs. It's still mostly dark when the first faint pink spot appears in the clouds. I lie within that brief interval of solitude just before the day advances, slow and red. A raven croaks.

Speaking of __

Let us lower our voices, said the woman next to me at the bus station; but I know what you are speaking of. Hammock strings have a way of recoiling. Is that when we can no longer lie in it? Then we might go indoors to make the meal, call the children in, unfold the blankets against the night's chill. Even so there will always be that one place you'll want to keep setting at the table, the room that will become a shrine. You'll never catalogue the growing things on that stretch of roadway, how many pieces of glass were rendered from the *kuatro kantos* bottle; what restraints might multiply in the hands of another. I am sorry too. Resemblance does not often matter. Money? Sex? It could have been a simple thing, the chrome of a radio dial sticking out of a jacket pocket. I listened this morning to stories of refugees trying to cross the Sahara; a woman's sobs woke me from sleep. From over the ridge, a patrolman's amplified voice, his words unintelligible. There are places in the world where a blue jay does his best impression of a red-tailed hawk, and then departs. Something like wings scissors in the sunlight. *Oh my poor poor sweetheart*, moans the woman in the desert, over and over again; *I could not even bury him.*

Consonance

Philavery /fil-a-vuh-ri/ n. An idiosyncratic collection of uncommon and pleasing words.

Unable to sleep till late (or early), I dithered
and tossed in the abstemious dark then clicked
on the lamp switch and sat up to read, finally
settling on my red-bound copy of Foyle's *Philavery*
(a present from my daughters two Christmases ago).
I'm not sure how it is that my mind drifted
to the issue of consonants—specifically those
that bump up in threes in the middle of words,
like castaways on an island. They sit shoulder
to shoulder and pass the coconut shell dipper
from hand to hand as they count sharks'
triangles in the morning and punched tin lights
overhead at night, having given up any real
hope for rescue. By then I'd begun to find more
and more of these words—like "cesssse", which
was the way some medieval 14th century texts
spelled what we know today as "ash"; or, more
familiar: "rhythm", "craftsmanship", and "ironclad"
(the latter reminding me of the Battleship Wisconsin,
berthed at the riverfront not even a quarter mile
from where we live). So when my husband, grumbling,
asked if I would like a ham sandwich (notice the three
consonants snug in the middle there, not even needing
any mustard or mayo), what could I do but nod my head
absently and muse aloud how it would be great if we had
some schnapps to go with that. While he was downstairs,
I'd drifted to Chelmno, a little town in Poland (its name
derives from an old Slavic word for hill), then wandered
some more afield, picking up a few hitch-hiking doubles
to keep company with the others: one sweet-talking
beekeeper, one slightly facetious bookkeeper, one gay
gypsy who'd been to Albuquerque. When morning
arrived, they marveled at the sight of a snowpack
glowing in soft light. I knew that a dog was barking
somewhere in the hills of Pennsylvania, and hoped he

would not cause an avalanche. When snow and ice melt,
they feed the rivers and the streams, but sometimes
cause flooding. You wake when you hear a resonant
knock in the dark, even though it could be only a woodpecker.
But then, it could also be the sound of a new door opening.

Jill McCabe Johnson

Jill McCabe Johnson has received the Paula Jones Gardiner Poetry Award, the *ScissorTale Review* Poetry Award, and four Pushcart nominations for her work in poetry, fiction, and nonfiction. She earned her MFA at Pacific Lutheran University, and is pursuing a PhD in English at the University of Nebraska. Her writing has been published in numerous journals including *The Los Angeles Review, Third Wednesday,* and *Harpur Palate*. She serves as an editorial assistant for *Prairie Schooner*, and is the editor of *Becoming*, an anthology of essays about the pivotal moments that transform women's lives.

Acknowledgments

"Honey, it's raining something terrible." appears in *Floating Bridge Review*

Sea Urge from Nebraska

Mornings I miss our North Shore walks,
bull kelp and sea lettuce drying on the rocks,
remnants of crab shells after plovers feed.

Each May, when Coast Tsimshian sun-bake seaweed
they press the purple laver, rockweed, and porphyra
into cakes for inland friends. In four days I can reach you

by car, though I started my walk months ago. Sea
lavender under the pillow. I step closer in my dreams.
Gather with me the cedar limbs anchored in the shallows

where herring eggs and sea palm lodge in the hollow mesh.
We'll drape madrona branches with the drying boughs,
then remind the children not to pluck rain flowers,

red columbine and bluebells blooming in the mallow. We'll listen
for the hesh-hesh-hesh of teeth shredding sea grass. We'll swim
through eelgrass meadows, wring heat from bonfire flames,

and I'll no longer miss those North Shore walks,
how your fingers cradled gifts of sea glass
nestled inside a mussel shell, coupled with byssal threads,
the way the sweat of sea salt lingered on my stomach and legs.

Honey, it's raining something terrible.

Waiting inside Best Buy for a downpour
of biblical immensity to subside, I phone
not because I miss you, but because I cannot recount for you

the look on the face of the policeman
who comes in hatless and soaked,
how he wipes rain from an 8 x 10 frame

before showing it to the store greeter
who shakes his head no.
Nor can I tell you the face in the picture

of the eleven or twelve year old boy, cheeks
round, skin flushed, and eyes whole.
Instead I say how the rain comes down in sheets,

how the pavement roils, and lightning makes
random stabs at us all.
The policeman tries to shield the frame

as he runs to the next store.
After he leaves, I watch how, discomposed,
the greeter tries to ignore

the paper with basic facts and number in red,
the way he squeezes his eyes closed,
and how slowly he shakes his head.

A Course around the Garden

He wrested foliage from a rhubarb stalk
and fanned himself with the blood-veined leaf.

Pretend someone murdered your son, he said.

He plucked blossoms from the foxglove
to encase my fingers' ends.

What would you do for revenge?

He stroked the umbel flowers,
and carved whistles from a water hemlock's stem.

I guess I would rely on the judicial system, I said.

He fingered the coral beads on my necklace,
and spoke of rosary peas tainted black.

What would you do, I asked him, *if you wanted revenge?*

He stepped over jack-in-the-pulpit's
low, triangulated heart.

Execution, he said, *can easily look like an accident...*

He led me through belladonna's
dusk of deathly nightshade.

...but I would let nature take its slow course.

Tina Kelley

Tina Kelley is on the staff of Covenant House, where she is co-writing a book about homeless teenagers to be published by Wiley in 2012. Her first book of poems, *The Gospel of Galore*, (Word Press, 2003) won a Washington State Book Award, and her second book, *Precise*, will be published by Word Press in 2012. She was a reporter at *The New York Times* for ten years, won a fraction of a Pulitzer Prize for being a part of the Times' coverage of the Sept. 11th attacks, and wrote 121 "Portraits of Grief," short descriptions of the victims. She lives with her husband and two children in Maplewood, NJ.

Acknowledgments

"Each of Us" appears in *Journal of New Jersey Poets*

Celebrations From The First Year In The New Country

The first firefly was caught, gilded, and placed around the neck
of the winner of the national essay contest on the importance of clarity.

We celebrated a bonfire of evergreens for the summer's first
sliver moon, and the most children nationwide were born

nine months later. There were carols to the one little creature
who so dearly wanted to be that she foiled two forms of birth control.

The katydids' cocktail party—blah blah blah across a thousand miles,
gossiping toe to toe, overlapping—conjured up our midnight picnics

of mead, peaches and browned butter, with sun-risen bread.
The land said "take, eat" with its bountiful berries.

Come fall, we enjoyed good junk day, exploring the neighborhood,
welcoming home discards. We granted wild amnesty, commemorated

the return of stolen goods, honored the owners. The thieves
cleaned up after our dogs all winter long. Late autumn

was given over to the memory of mountain huckleberries,
a mile from any path, never picked, their tiny fermentation,

and the staggering bears who loved them. The shortest
day was devoted to friendship with god, planning a menu

fit for a creator. The day after the solstice, ten teenaged fire jugglers
started chin deep, wading with a new anthem, sunrising from the sea.

Each spring we wrote a new creation myth, in which the female
is always made first. We sang to the Birds Who Always Fly,

asking them to nest here in this well-storied land. We who were scattered
to get here, as scattered as the roots that grew this bonfire's driftwood,

threw seeds, like candy from a parade. At dusk, the wet air smelling
of solace, the peepers loosened, and the baby year softened down to sleep.

Christened Christina, Now Fran

"Mafiosi have whores and loose women," he says. "But lovers? No." A real lover might make demands and expect someone who is more than a brutal cog in a corporation of unfettered allegiance. And that, LoVerso explains, "causes a crisis, because if you love and are loved, you have a name."
~ from a profile of Girolamo LoVerso, psychoanalyst studying the love lives of the mob, The New York Times, August 24, 2002

I had to love wildly, like a kite flying
til the string soars out,
the abandon and abundance of that.

And I had a weakness for bold men. They were black umbrellas,
huge with solid wooden handles, inscribed with a fancy brand,
so wide and deep I felt like some rich gentleman in his fifties

had sheltering arms around me as I walked in pouring rain.
And he did. Believe me when I say it was late when he told me
what he did for a living. Killing.

I couldn't understand. It was like reading
letters blurring by, twigs in front of the full moon
fast, seen from the limo's back seat.

The portrait he commissioned of me,
its eyes look steeped in formaldehyde.
He ordered the brass plaque, Untitled.

I wonder. He was afraid of butterflies when he was little.
He grew near the broken windows of his father's care.
Christ, it was his idea to take home those kittens.

~

I think of the awful white explosions from hard-boiled eggs.
I think of snow blowing in spirals, creating itself up
from nothing, then sinking down. I think of ghosts

in a burglarized house. How often do surnames die out?
I will forget his, one letter at a time. First I will forget
the sex names we had for those times. I'll forget how

if he talked sweet, he looked like he was speaking a second language.
I'll forget his torso, shiny as snot, when we lay down to sleep, spent.
Francisco, Francis, the saint who would not blow out a candle

for fear of hurting the flame. Words sound hollow pointed.
I am listening through a balloon. "Carve your name
on your heart and not on marble" was our last fortune cookie.

"Unidentified female (decomposed)
found on roof" – the last police report.
I ran. I hid. My name had not stuck to much.

I found a new one. New town, job, numbers. I kept a list
of all the things I ever lost, the gold cross, Raggedy Ann,
plane ticket home from Chicago. The first 27 years. Frankie.

Done Procreating

With this new beginning there's a certain end to things.
No more happy visits to the hospital, ever.
No more knowledge of the shortness and sureness of healing,
no more announcements to all friends of good news,
never again. Is this the happiest we will ever be, will
we look back wistfully and say, ah, that was the year
the children were so young, and all was so hopeful, trust unstained?
Loss takes over the tell-all-friends news: the folks selling
the family homestead, the dog, the cat put down after outlasting
seven romances, the inevitable deaths now there's to be
no more birthing. I'll never do a handstand while nine months
pregnant. Each milestone is the Last new baby trick,
last first smiling, last first laughing. Clothes outgrown
won't be worn again in this house. And who would fall for me
now, cut off from all old flames who showed signs of peskiness,
bruisy rings under my eyes from the 5 a.m. feeding, impy haircut
requiring no grooming time, since I have none. Last maternity
leave, no plans to move to a new house, no chance of travel. But

I love his little blueberry eyes, such a dark gray, and when
I looked in them last night I could see how I look to him—
my pale skin out of the hole in the black nursing bra, then my head
and behind it, the headboard. In Drew's little world, where
every square foot, every three-hour wakening is new, his smile
travels high into his scalp, and fills the room deep like a ghost.

Each Of Us

By the time it is done growing there are about a billion billion water molecules in a typical snowflake, Dr. Libbrecht says. And on average, he calculates, each of us on Earth has contributed by exhalation and evaporation about 1,000 of the molecules in each snowflake.
~ The New York Times, December 23, 2003

We are all here in these eyelashes of flakes zinging at our faces over and over,
our loves requited and not, the joyful young man I wrote to the summer after college,

and Trisha, who said, "I fell in love with a Japanese woman who was making teeth,"
and the man who tried to record all the shapes of all the clouds ever,

and the man who felt sentenced to life, accused of abusing a child,
because killing himself would appear an admission of guilt.

Here's the woman who wrote the slogan "Cat bathing made easy!"
and the nurse who said of newborns, "They're all cartilage." I see Ella,

like a carousel horse, impaled on her fear, lurching forward a bit, inevitably
retreating. I want her to break free of whatever darkness constrains her.

I see the drunk woman who called the operator three times demanding to talk to her father
in Tennessee. And here's the owner of a diamond lost on the Broadway sidewalk.

Here's the dad who says "Smile and say pumpernickel" before taking a picture,
and here is the man whose eyes were so dark, no one could see his pupils.

There is the child who, from a few months' old, would hold on to his mother's earlobe
whenever he got tired. And newlyweds who fit together like notes and measures.

I notice a few molecules from the man who bought his late wife's favorite perfume
to spray it on his pillow before he went to bed, the only way he could sleep.

~

And the guy who wanted to write a poem starring the moon, without the word moon in it.
And Em's friend composing a song, "Sorry for the Things I Did to You in Your Dream."

Here's the 98-year-old woman who was born with wrinkled hands. The doctor
said she must've had all her troubles in a previous life, and looking back, she agreed.

And a man who wanted his ashes put in a figurehead of a ship, thinking the bowsprit's the best place for traveling the ocean for the rest of time.

Thousands of thousands of molecules melt on me, maybe including saints and my late grandmothers. Come along, look up, mouth open. Take them in, a cold wet eucharist.

Janet Norman Knox

Seven-time Pushcart nominee and 2007 finalist for the Discovery/The Nation Award, Janet Norman Knox's poems have appeared in *Los Angeles Review, Crab Creek Review, Rhino, Diner, Seattle Review, Adirondack Review, Poetry Southeast, Cranky Literary Journal, Red Mountain Review,* and *Diagram*. Her chapbook, *Eastlake Cleaners When Quality & Price Count [a romance]* received the Editor's Choice Award. She received the 2008 Ruskin Poetry Prize (Red Hen Press) and read with Molly Peacock and Paul Muldoon. *The Los Angeles Review* nominated her for 2010 Best New Poets.

Acknowledgments

"Night Art" appears in *Los Angeles Review*
"Cocooned, White Sheets, Slip Feet" appears in *Pontoon*
"Gravity Dog" appears in *Rhino*

Gravity Dog

First, let's talk about what
we know. We know dust
is roughly 95% human
dander depending on the number
of household pets. We know
dander is dead skin,
we know dead skin
is a raft of genetic
stuff, elementary DNA, Watson

and Crick. Seriously, let's talk
about not knowing where
the exosphere ends and space
begins, the white and black
of it, the line between them
and us or us and nothing.

Finally, let's talk about
what can happen there, where
we thin into nothing,
exposed to radiation,
no pressure or friction.

I know, you say most of the dust
has settled by now, but there
must be a mite of dust wafting
where atoms speed up,
escaping earth's gravity.
Is that where DNA
is being copied,
cloned dust merging
with solar wind?
If only a minute
particle of you
would fall back
to earth, a new
you might grow,
you and your dog.

Night Art

Will I regret not calling into the night—not running half
clad to check if you are there—safe across the tree tops
a barn owl calls—wait—finds a mate in the quiet of dead
middle night when the making of art can take all this—all
the midnight light, all the nocturne noise, even the bats
have folded away behind banana leaves, even the heat
cicadas their singing ribs—tymbals like cymbals lie still
and airless even the frogs painted in poison—cadmium
red, Chinese yellow, Parrot green—mouth a mute
meditation to the work of art that night itself is without
the stretch of canvas, without the itch of bowdrill pen
to spark—half mad and haunted by night
art, hiding in a blaring chorus of imagines so thick
a hush I slice with one ear to hear a word working
its way against paper—catching a scrape of your palate
knife, a whiff of beeswax, a touch of your tongue?

Imagines (Latin plural of imago): 1. *Entomology.* adult cicadas; 2. *Psychoanalysis.* idealized concepts of a loved one, formed in childhood and retained unaltered in adult life.

Cocooned, White Sheets, Slip Feet

A moth slow-flapping glides,
the blaze of moon on lake.

Our pull of oar. Dip. Slide.
A pace that will not break.

The blaze of moon on lake,
your eyes in mine you row

the pace that will not break,
obsidian sky below.

Your eyes in mine you row,
the sight of shore now lost

obsidian deep below
the reach of moonflame crossed.

Our sight of shore now lost,
drop oar, two bodies meet.

the reach of moonflame crossed,
cocooned, white sheets, slip feet.

Drop oar, two bodies meet.
The pull of oar. White sheets.

Cocooned, a moth
slow-flapping glides.

Keetje Kuipers

Keetje Kuipers is a native of the Northwest. She earned her B.A. at Swarthmore College and her M.F.A. at the University of Oregon. In 2007 she completed her tenure as the Margery Davis Boyden Wilderness Writing Resident, which provided her with seven months of solitude in Oregon's Rogue River Valley. She used her time there to complete work on her book, *Beautiful in the Mouth*, which was awarded the 2009 A. Poulin, Jr. Poetry Prize and was published in March 2010 by BOA Editions. Keetje has taught writing at the University of Montana and is currently a Wallace Stegner Fellow at Stanford University. At the moment, she divides her time between San Francisco and Missoula, Montana, where she lives with her dog, Bishop, and does her best to catch a few fish.

Acknowledgments

"The Keys to the Jail" appears in *The Northwest Review*
"Wolf Season" appears in *Barrow Street*
"I Will Away" appears in *The Rumpus*
"Sometimes a Season Changes Overnight" appears in *Tar River Poetry*

Wolf Season

My past apart from yours is a landscape
governed by false erasure of snow:
fence-lines pin drifts in their barbed hold,
animals abandon their tracks behind them.

This is why I tire easily in your presence.
Your press is the weight of so much crushing
touch that's come before, each layer
half-melted and refrozen above me.

Even in this unfamiliar city—odd to us as soap
passed between tongues, where the radio tower tilts
like a lost ship's mast, the train rounding
each corner one section at a time, body trailing

somewhere behind the head—I'm sealed
beneath. Your naked back bent over
the wilderness of bathroom tiles as you
wash yourself at my sink is last winter's

buffalo turned from me and halted in the snow.
In that country I left behind, they're hunting wolves.
What never changes feels most new—
your hand on my wrist, the sound of a gun.

The Keys to the Jail

It's the second day of spring.
In Montana, we burn our garbage.
Two blocks down, the Dairy Queen
swings open its shutters for another
season. We tell our sad stories
until the dog hangs his head
in the wet snow-wells of the too-soon
tulips. It gets uglier every year:
The same melt that clears the gutters
uncovers the dead, or the not-dead-
long-enough. And suddenly
we smell them again, their bodies
unlocked from that frozen state
of decay, the mouths slack
but whispering, their cold breath
fresh on the air. Except the breath
is our own, the voices belong
to you and me, and the music they make
is not the swift tumble of locks,
but the drop of bones in a bowl.

Sometimes a season changes overnight

Flat-top clouds are tacked above the highway
where it seems the hands of invisible children
push yellow trucks and winking cars
along the blacktop toward a skylight of snow,
small cheeks puffed to push engine breath
between their lips. Your real children run
the corn field maze, eighteen-wheelers
shuddering past. You watch them move the dry sheaves
like bangles tossed up a long, thin wrist.
Not yet November and roadside pumpkins
appear as if pulled from a hat, the iced streets
still filled with girls on cold bicycles, metal tight
between their legs. You layer sweater
over sweater and ask yourself, when
did I stop being one of those girls on a bike,
a bridge just a way of getting somewhere faster?
This morning you pulled the shirt off
over your head to find the very weight of your breasts
had made the pale spokes of a wheel on your skin,
stretch marks raying from the nipple, the way a bullet
hole through a window can look like a star. What
was her name—that girl you kissed so long ago—
and where is her twin body now, the pear-shaped
silence still held between you, her form lit by what lamp
in what room out of sight, underground,
in what winter cellar just across the state line?

I Will Away

With your promises tucked
like a dry newspaper
under my safe arm.
While the televisions play
their favorite ode to cops and robbers
and the sodium lights sing
I-am-orange all over town.
I will away like the BB-gunned
bird, the .22ed squirrel:
limping, half-wrecked, and visibly
alive. I will away the midnight
jogger, passing shadowed rooms
of fuchsia and cold furnaces,
where unbidden ears count
the ticking of water heaters
against the uncertain clock
of someone else's wood smoke,
the shoveling of someone else's snow.
I will away ivy, not the vine,
dead dog, not the frozen
tennis ball in his mouth;
I will away a light bulb crushed
without a handkerchief and the dull
glass swept from your house.

Dorianne Laux

Dorianne Laux's most recent collections are *The Book of Men* and *Facts about the Moon*. A finalist for the National Book Critics Circle Award, and winner of the Oregon Book Award, Laux is also author of *Awake*, *What We Carry*, and *Smoke* from BOA Editions, as well as a fine press edition, *Dark Charms* from Red Dragonfly Press. She teaches poetry in the MFA Program at North Carolina State University and is founding faculty at Pacific University's Low Residency MFA Program.

Acknowledgments

"Superman" appears in *Superman: The Chapbook*
(Red Dragonfly Press, 2008)
"How to Sleep" appears in *River Styx Magazine*
"Timing" appears in *American Poetry Review*
"Sunday" appears in *Awake* (BOA Editions, Ltd., EWU Press, Carnegie Mellon Press, 2011)

Superman

Superman sits on a tall building
smoking pot, holding the white plumes in,
palliative for the cancerous green glow
spreading its tentacles beneath his
blue uniform, his paraffin skin.

The pot also calms him so he can look
down through the leafy crowns of the Trees
of Heaven to patches of black asphalt
where a small dog chained to a grate
raises his leg against a sapling.

It's 2010 and the doctors have given him
another year in Metropolis. Another year
in paradise when he's high, another year
in hell when he's not.
A magazine falls from his lap. Lois
on the cover of *Fortune*, the planets
aligned behind her, starlight glancing off
her steely upswept hair.

He lifts his head from his hands
as the sun sets, the sound of muffled gunfire
in every city of the world ricochets
through his gray brain. He'll take care of it
tomorrow, the thankless, endless task
of catching dirty bombs and bullets,
though like the dishes piling up in the sink
there are always more.

365 dark days left to try to gather them all,
tunnel through to the earth's core
and bury them there. But for now he leans
his wide back against the stove-hot bricks
and stretches each long blue leg.
Blissfully stoned he doesn't notice
when his heel clips the chipped wing
of a granite angel, can't feel the Kryptonite
bending its rays up toward his scarlet heart.

Sunday
after Wallace Stevens

We sit on the front lawn, an igloo
cooler between us. So hot, the sky
is white. Above the gravel rooftops
a spire, a shimmering cross.

You pick up the swollen hose, press
your thick thumb into the silver nozzle.
A fan of water sprays rainbows
over the dying lawn. Hummingbirds

sparkle green. Bellies powdered
with pollen from the bottle-brush tree.
The bells of twelve o'clock.
Our neighbors return from church.

I bow my head as they ease
clean cars into neat garages, file
through screen doors in lace gloves,
white hats, Bible-black suits.

The smell of barbeque rises, hellish
thick and sweet. I envy their weekly
peace of mind. They know
where they're going when they die.

Charcoal fluid cans contract in the sun.
I want to be Catholic. A Jew. Maybe
a Methodist. I want to kneel
for days on rough wood.

Their kids appear in bright shorts,
bathing suits, their rubber thongs
flapping down the hot cement.
They could be anyone's children;

they have God inside their tiny bodies.
My god, look how they float, like birds

through the scissor-scissor-scissor
of lawn sprinklers.

Down the street, a tinny radio bleats.
The sun bulges above our house
like an eye. I don't want to die.
I never want to leave this block.
I envy everything, all of it. I know

it's a sin. I love how you can shift
in your chair, take a deep drink
of gold beer, curl your toes under, and hum.

Timing

Ah, timing. Woody Allen says
it's everything. I say it's nothing,
can't touch it, wear it, hold it up
between your fingers and shake it
like a napkin. Timing is what you have
when you don't have anything else,
a facility with the wine list, a joke
that hits the bull's eye in the spongy
marrow of a funny bone. Or death,
that takes timing too, to elude,
you must bend to pick up the fork
you nervously, clumsily dropped
so the bullet that whizzed through the wall
from the shop next door where a man
of few words was holding up
a terrified clerk lost his balance
for a moment and the gun went off,
the bullet marked to end the next thought
in your roundly specific head sailing
straight through the window, shattering
the harmless glass, nicking the letter D
on the marquee across the street, a movie
you meant to see after dinner with a woman
who could become your wife, but who now
looks at you as if you are a wanted man, a man
with a foreseeable future, though not
in the way you had hoped.

How To Sleep

Let your mountainous forehead
with its veins of bright ore
ease down, the deep line
between your brow flatten,
unruffle the small muscles
below your temples, above
your jaws, let the grimace
muscles in your cheekbones
go, the weeping muscles
sealing your eyes. Die into
the pillow, calm in the knowledge
that you will someday cease, soon
or late, late or soon, the song
you're made of will stop, your body
played out, the currents pulsing
through your brain drained
of their power, their purpose,
will frizzle out through
your fingertips, private sparks
leaping weakly onto the sheets
where you lie breathing
and then not breathing.
Lay your head down and relax
into it: death. Accept it.
Trick yourself like this.
Hover in a veil of ethers.
Call it sleep.

Jenifer Browne Lawrence

Jenifer Browne Lawrence is the author of *One Hundred Steps from Shore* (Blue Begonia, 2006). She was awarded the 2011 James Hearst Poetry Prize for her poem, "What Her Father Cast" and is a Washington State Artist Trust GAP grant recipient. Her work appears in *Bellevue Literary Review, Crab Creek Review, Court Green, Narrative,* the *North American Review* and elsewhere. Jenifer serves on the Centrum advisory board for the Port Townsend Writers' Conference.

Acknowledgments

"Three for the OB Clinic" appears in *Bellevue Literary Review*

Poppies in the Garden, Sugar in the Bed

she says, and tips a dry pod
into her pocket.
He won't miss a few seeds.

These petals crinkle
like crepe paper, pink,

big as a teacup.
She presses seeds
into my palm, stops

to pinch
a stem of begonia, snip

a drying agapanthus
as we walk the streets
in her neighborhood.

They'll see you, Mother,
I whisper, and she nods,

silver hair brushing her cheek,
pockets full of what
she's stolen on my behalf.

Three for the OB Clinic

Night is a Tent

Above the cat-track river,
branches twine like women
arm in arm. Courage is not

astronomical, the moon is

a walleyed fish gawping
surface air in the chink of light
the sky bleeds out like milt.

Tree the Color of Winter-Loved Skin

Speak to us in ghost light.
Drum the instinct of fall, squirrel
away blind fancy, fat
braids combed through with moss.
Strew our paths with decomposing,
in this wood made of shadow,
this cadence of sparrow,
this nurse log, hollow as our hands.

Key Fruit

Golden moths a moment before
flight, maple seeds
hang in clusters, resist
fertility in the damp
earth, slow sink
to germination,
the five-striped chipmunk
waiting for wings to fall.
Leaves twirl like spent wishes.
All month we've kept
a banked fire in the woodstove,
not blazing heat but stoked embers,
a ritual gleaned from wood.

Elegy for a Jar of Cured Salmon Eggs in the Giant's Creel

i.

I don't love you, the boy
tells his father,

punctuating each word
with a red plastic hammer.

ii.

His hands cradling the trout:
tip of the pocketknife

pushed into its belly,
blade drawn to the jaw.

iii.

Here is a peace sign stretched into a coat hanger.

iv.

He is a sprung mousetrap.
Clay tiles
pried loose by the wind.

A Swiss Army knife with all its tools
opened.

v.

Trying
to slip into a pocket.

Kate Lebo

Kate Lebo's poems have appeared in *Poetry Northwest, Bateau, Crab Creek Review* and other journals. She's an associate poetry editor for *Filter,* a literary journal made entirely by hand, and she lives in Seattle, where she worked for Richard Hugo House for many years. In 2010 she was awarded a grant from 4Culture, a Soapstone residency, and a Shotpouch Creek residency. This year she's an MFA candidate at the University of Washington. For more about Kate's zine, *A Commonplace Book of Pie*, and other tasty treats, visit her blog Good Egg:
www.goodeggseattle.blogspot.com

Acknowledgments

"Day Trip to Vashon With Heather" appears in *DMQ Review*
"Happy Birthday" appears in *Poetry Northwest*

Day Trip to Vashon with Heather

Noon feels like a nectarine.
You toss it to me underhanded,

just like the girl you once were,
then raise your camera

to shoot the field abloom
in my dress.

Proof! Our troubles
are similar.

We are like that motorhome
posted for sale on the thru road:

Gorgeous inside!
Affordable!

You want your pictures
to make monuments of us;

I want to look serene as a still life
of salt shakers. This

is a Saturday feeling.
Through your lens

sunlight is semaphore blurted
by cedars, messages

I uncrypt easily. They say
the joyful half of hunger

makes eating
our dividend of daytime.

Appetite can hide
in a napkin, a grass spear,

a coffee stain. They say I
am an oven. My heart bakes bread

for a lifetime of lovehandles.
That you will never not love

eating pop rocks off your palm
or losing Seattle in the small

of the sea. Our lives
are livable. Forgivable!

Affordable
as this breath of air.

Redeye

Salt dark curves under a circle of dawn,
the lit shore. Below,

water ferries nails from wood,
shoes from feet, deep from deep from
can't get to sleep. That's me waving,

my window speeding through the cloudsmear
your eye wanted to plug with a full moon.

Our plane is made of heartbeats over water,
the whir of beaten air, assumptions about land

that demand an upright and locked position.
We count the knots in God's cold net

of ocean, worry our ginger ale and foresee,
for the duration of flight, only one way
of dying on fire while drowning by surprise.

Ground temperature is Tuesday,
48 degrees and raining, the day as near
as I am to my neighbor's elbow,

our purchase on the armrest a territory
lifetimes across and divisible by sleeves, skin
too close to imagine, in the dim cabin just
a shrug of light.

Happy Birthday

Another November
off my list. What's left?
Damp laundry, your
hesitating kiss.
My egg breath
and shoehorn thighs.
I've leaned your name
in my mouth
like a rake,
and tallied all
the dependable
things:

tap water, junk mail,
the rough shade you cast
when I turn my head just so
to the left, the rag
stuffed beneath my dish rack,
half-black and blurred as a rubbed eye,
the stains bearding the bathroom
window and the sky.

I'm still renting my pay from the city.
Still reading the *Times*
like a barcode. No smarter
than I started,
but no more guilty than a bathrobe.

Duty is still my body
catching the 49 bus,
patience is the paint chip
in the white kitchen wall
where a square of red
blinks like a brake light
and habit,

if we have it,
is your toothbrush drying

in the short plastic cup.
Behind the house a hubbub
of rhubarb
doubles down under the dirt. Your tomatoes
are as green as green grows.

Carol Levin

Carol Levin is the author of chapbooks: *Sea Lions Sing Scat* (Finishing Line Press) *Red Rooms and Others* (Pecan Grove Press) and a full volume due 2012, *Stunned By the Velocity* (Pecan Grove Press). As former Literary Manager for The Art Theater of Puget Sound she translated Chekhov's plays. She's an Editorial Assistant at *Crab Creek Review* and teaches The Breathing Lab / Alexander Technique, in Seattle.
www.the-breathing-lab.com/about/poetry/

Acknowledgments

"The Most Important Thing to Save When the House is Burning Down" appears in *Red Rooms and Others* (Pecan Grove Press, 2009)
"Souvenir Shards" appears in *Stunned By the Velocity* (forthcoming, Pecan Grove Press , 2012)

Souvenir Shards

Memory flutters like heatwaves above asphalt
and it's futile to interrogate memory. I distrust
memory.

Remember
Chios—ages ago? An island in Greece
wavering seven sea miles

from the grimy village of Cesme, Turkey.
I still see blue sky and sea under sun and wind
on a motor launch to the island's white harbor,

my car broadside hanging
out across the stern. I don't remember
how we docked or the morning ride

sixty miles over mountains to the outpost
of Emborios. Today it is a Port, there
is a little dock, still a black rock beach, footprints

of my children washed long ago away.
Must be electric light now,
there are apartments to rent. Is there nothing

left that I remember? The migrant workers
stooping in the sun to tap Mastica trees'
sap for gum? Where are Hermionie
and Yergos Polykronopolis—
their traditional handmade house, the precious

propane lamps they commanded
us to protect, then smashed against
the stairs.

I don't deny ducking lethal threats
they threw at me echoing
off their cool walls,

the sound dying away the faster
I drove in wavy light, a long way

away by car, ferry, plane, time.

They didn't try to follow
but they left themselves behind
in the black rock, serene sea and mountain
landscape for me to remember
and that is the tyranny of memory.

The Strangest Things Remind Me of Me

Immediately after.
And still, the morning
after

startled into
spikes, after
it's severed.

Settled after splashes
of shampoo
soothe and tame

raw battered
cuticle tips
to punctuate gloss

after fate's
rapid growth
invigorates the halo.
White hair
snippits floating

floorward
unleashed
like the day

I resigned
walked away,
after

co-workers
young, and gung-ho
whispered

wellwishes
thinking good
riddance.

I cheered, relieved, let

them lie. Left,
in jobs

just dead
ends.

The Most Important Thing to Save When the House is Burning Down

Save George. Save the way he says *bow wow*
as he greets his crush of dogs.
Save how he rolls on the floor three dogs
clambering over him licking his beard.
How he laughs and how all four of them
make those snuggling noises.
Save George when he is excited
and lifts his heels bobbing
off the floor, sometimes
drops of spittle sparkle in the corner
of his lips while he tells stories
and can't talk fast enough.
His cut hands are calloused,
raw from working wood.
Save the way he looks at them and shrugs.
Save George who never looks at dirt,
the worst person to clean house.
You can save him regardless—
as you follow him around to find
what messes he misses—
but watch, he can't pass
the coffee table without setting
each item in the spot
he insists it must be. Methodically
he moves the Deco birchwood box
an eighth of an inch, straightens
the album, exacting edge to edge.
Don't forget
to save the way he walks room
to room brushing his teeth.
Even if you find the toothbrush
abandoned on the kitchen counter or top
of the dresser, save it.
He is a hugger.
That is the most important thing to save
when the house is burning down.
Save his hugs and how, when he hugs,
he says—that's nice
I needed that.

Rebecca Loudon

Rebecca Loudon lives and writes in Seattle. Her most recent book is *Cadaver Dogs* published by No Tell Books. She is currently working on a collection of poems titled *Queer Wing-ed* about the inner life of the artist Henry Darger. Rebecca is a professional musician and teaches violin lessons to children.

A rip in the syncope

Language clogged my mouth I said
I am bit by spiders every night
My clothes never dried damp
With damp stink damp intentions
A history of knives up my sleeve
There was no room for jealousy
You ate the Christmas lights
Prayerful and dangerous
Described my demon like an animal
Freeing itself from a toothy trap
You set aside a bowl of oranges
A monstrous cork a primer
For madness and now I am crying
Telling you about this monumental
Voice in my head which never manages
To end *the wrong voice*
I am stubborn
I am a liar

a fraction of a degree in the delicious thin

I ran with desire
ran with a ball gag in my mouth

ran out of that dry slut town
casseroles and salads

all the soldiers smiled
your father might have been

a dentist so damaged were you
in the autoclave

who hangs on you now
the devil yelled in my head

like Fats Waller
Bedbug's big as a jackass

will bite you and stand and grin
I knelt in a tent

the psalm maker made it grow
men in starched white shirts

butterfly funnel
cleave knot

crisp white shirts
that smelled

that smelled
like Jesus

deranged people entered and I thought they were angels

I discovered your artifacts
sprawled across my map
the autistic child
flamingo inflamed face
colitis any child-
hood disease even polio
to keep the train moving
in an eastern direction
this morning I folded
towels warm from the dryer
found a letter with oddly
dotted eyes a girl's eyes
a girl with a crush
making her way backward
from cloth to paper to lint
I barely twitched
wished you calamity
and ill fortune

coil your scaly tail right down the street brother I am tired collapsed burning damping burning damping my window open for the world to watch if it kneels if it crawls low enough it can see clear to the meadow rabbits ears pressed back building their Easter diorama their vinegar hole

empty head empty head empty head
the truth about New Orleans
is I had history there too
you denied my breast
in the elevator the river's brown stink
your pearly egg on end nipples leaking
as Napoleon counted spoons at St. Helena
we sought lesser saints

Saint Diphtheria
Saint Eczema
Saint Genital Herpes

stuffed newspapers into your shoes stuck with a boy's milk-voice I never really wanted to know you I could have been your mother in a gravy-spattered housecoat but I lack the instinct that keeps us from devouring our children their pink pink meat sweet as decay or an infestation of bedbugs any illness that mimics a hillside covered with sweetpeas

a letter twisted in the tide pools
among jellyfish spider crabs sand fleas
bees hovered over the woman's body
I don't forgive
I have as much forgiveness in me as a cat

the godhead pushed deeper than you imagined and we could not stop eating you were the noise maker in the monastery only my kitchen betrayed me water sprung from the tap as bees hovered over meat gone bad

I found a poison that slapped you down
don't say a thing was key
I am diminished for having known you
for having taught you how to make the Queen
you stole all the royal jelly for yourself

On Tour with *The Billy Tipton Saxophone Quartet*

A woman walked toward me
stuck her fingers in her eyes
to avoid looking
it's like playing piano she said
(that easy)
like playing Bach she said
(that easy)
or running with a broken champagne flute
in your mouth
easypeasy she said.
I rubbed the hairy wen on my left wrist.

It pained me to think of his constricted chest the muscle pull yet I would gleefully take hot tongs to his tongue nothing worse than feeling duped than waking up to cold meat and beer. The Portuguese boy in the cigarette factory lopped off his thumb he said *I'm no performing monkey* when the ambulance drove away lights pulsing as cuckoo-shrikes rose from the mud to announce their lack of water.

Darfur water conflict.
Tibet water conflict.
Sudan water conflict.
Water stressed countries.

The next day I discovered a velvet bag in a chicken pot pie. I was not the best hostess. I had to play *Snow White* in Port Townsend that night. I wore paper slippers the blue and yellow dress my skin white as an egg. I rode the ferry first car at the prow. I let down the chain let down the wedges at my front wheels let down my pinched bodice let down my windows and slid into the Pacific Ocean.

Erin Malone

Erin Malone's poems have appeared in journals such as *Field, Beloit Poetry Journal, POOL* and online at *Verse Daily*. Her chapbook, *What Sound Does It Make*, won the Concrete Wolf Award in 2007. The recipient of grants from Washington's Artist Trust, 4Culture and the Colorado Council of the Arts, she has taught writing at the University of Colorado in Colorado Springs, Richard Hugo House in Seattle, and at the University of Washington Rome Center in Italy. She currently teaches poetry in Seattle Arts & Lectures' Writers in the Schools program. www.erinmalone.com

Acknowledgments

"Invocation" and "*And None of Mine Own*" appear in *What Sound Does It Make* (Concrete Wolf, 2008)
"Classifications of Languages" appears online at *Rattapallax*

And None of Mine Own

When I went, I went west
until there was no more. Forsook
the eastern cities and seaboard, shied the lights

for stars. I addressed my west as darling.
My west is a boy with a bucket

of beach on his arm: won't dress
for dinner or come when he's called.

Won't listen. Wears antlers.
I asked my west how best to hold him
but lost his answer

among the rocks he skipped across the lake.
My west is a narrow stretch

longed for. He whittles trees
to teeth and feeds them to a bone-filled fire.
I followed him like a trail

but oh my west is merciless, a boy
who leaves as I left with light on his back,
an arrow of grief in his heel.

Invocation

O potato, freckled-in-rows-of-four-where-forked
Heart, so dogged, so dog-like, bumping & literal,
And the brain who thinks it's better, my scheming
Separatist brain, my hoarder, hunched accordionist
How I've hated you, no less & no more than
My automatic lungs—wait, now, wait, now—
Hate the mouth asking *How many times have I told you?*
What language am I speaking? Shut up. Curse you:
I repeat, & this skin I shed but am not rid of, to this shaped
Rubber glove skin, a curse. A curse on the hands
Which had not & wanted, which had & did not want.
Curse my arms: I have flung him. I have held him down.
Curse my fingers: button-pushers, bruisers, crooks.
Curse the good ear who listened when the voice insisted
What kind of mother? Are you?—O, but bless
The deaf one, who scans for signs & still responds
To touch, to shadows that align like birds above the water.
Bless my arms: I gather him. Bless my hands, their strokes.
Bless the legs who kick to save themselves, & all right yes
This whole damned lot—gristle, tongue & stuffing, fat
Balloons, the eyes' horizon—& god help you,
Bless you, unlovely thudding pump, who sinks & sinks
And bobs back up

Classifications of Languages

Those directed at the sky
Those that star and underline

Those that are cross
            Holes torn in paper, half-erased

Ones that "never endeavor to advocate"

Those that confuse instructions and destructions
Those that drop objects

            All thumbs

Dead ones

Those that explain photosynthesis of phytoplankton
            in metagenomics
Those that are made up

Those that make up
Those that are enduringly dirty

Ones that say how do you like them apples
            Say sorry I burned the goddamn pastry

Round-mouthed ones calling

            Those that walk, imprinting the snow

Those that lobtail
Those that lobby for the protection of the Island Marble Butterfly
            and old-world parlors

Those meaning mother
Those that lie down in the dark with a light

Those that swell
Those that whisper Salish Sea, Salish Sea

Marjorie Manwaring

Marjorie Manwaring lives in Seattle, where she is a freelance writer/editor and co-editor of the online poetry and art journal the *DMQ Review* (www.dmqreview.com). Her work has most recently appeared in *Willow Springs, Floating Bridge Review*, and the anthology *New Poets of the American West*, and her chapbook *What to Make of a Diminished Thing* will be published by Dancing Girl Press in 2012. www.mmanwaring.com

Acknowledgments

"Charm" appears in the *2010 Jack Straw Writers Anthology*
"Rejection Letter from Gertrude Stein" appears in the *DMQ Review* and was reprinted in *Pontoon: An Anthology of Washington State Poets, No. 7*

Charm

Automatic doors seal shut, the air artificial and cool. Thick with the smell of a deep fat fryer, fresh butchered meat, bananas just out of cold storage. Mom gets a cart. You linger in this alcove of news racks and gumball machines, one filled with Chiclets, one with jawbreakers big as golf balls, and this one, the one that dazzles you, its display card alive with trinkets and plastic charms… You align your dime into its special slot. Crank the metal handle. The mound of treasure shifts, a small upheaval, and you hear the plastic capsule sliding down the chute. Will it be a tiny bird whistle—yellow, orange, or baby blue—that when filled halfway with water and blown will chirp and warble? Or the salmon-pink Cupid with his sideways glance, bow drawn back, one leg flexed behind him? These would please you, held tightly in your hand or worn on a chain, but the miniature magnifying glass—something small that lets you see things even smaller, this is what you want, what you need and you already see yourself sliding it in and out of its little red sheath.

Thinking About Someone I Used To Love

It makes me sad because I've never seen such—such beautiful shirts before.
~ Daisy Buchanan, from F. Scott Fitzgerald's *The Great Gatsby*

Is it overly romantic
to want to see
through *spectacles,* not *glasses,*
to wish the sign
on the door read
oculist instead of
ophthalmologist,
to desire a man
who owns a stack
of long-sleeved dress shirts,
to cradle those linens and silks,
to brush their luxury,
their meticulous weaves
across your lips,
to feel pleasure as you
watch him hold
your favorite—periwinkle
—the one with nearly invisible
pink flecks, imagine
what he's thinking as he slides
each arm into its sleeve,
pops each button
into place, pats down his front
and tucks the hem into pleated
unbelted trousers?
You wonder if he wonders
about words, how they can change
everything, East Egg
to West Egg and back again,
the distance, far and not far,
between the valley of ashes
and this place, where at dusk
the gulls call madly
as the city lights up the sound.
Is it foolish to mourn
the eras of elegance
and danger that have passed

you by and will you
take this chance
at love, a gangster
with a wardrobe full of shirts,
because aren't all men invented,
riffraff still clinging to the bottom
of their shoes, and isn't he a man
who promises, promises, and
won't you choose
to believe him?

Le Pichet

The waiter fills my cup
with a strong dark brew

brings cream in a small
white pitcher

—size you might find
in a tea set for dolls.

I pour, stir in the cool
rich antidote to bitter.

Clack of the silver spoon. . .
intimate space of the cafe. . .

my hands wrapped around something hot
filling some kind of domestic lack.

Across the street
there's a women's boutique.

So chic the mannequin
has no head, wears

a yellow plaid swing coat
meant to drape softly across shoulders

that are bony and sharp.
The neck a sort of stump, knob

on a closed door. Abrupt—
like how things ended between us.

The waiter's returned
with my order—eggs broiled

with Gruyère and ham.
A plate of crusty bread.

More coffee, ramekin

of butter. That coat. . .

I bet it moves gracefully in the wind
but wonder if it keeps a person very warm.

Rejection Letter From Gertrude Stein

Dear Poet Dear Author Dear Someone:

We are pleased very pleased
To regret sir.
Regret to inform you the list for
Talents selected not you dear.
So many many and many
Many talents not you dear.
Received many fine not you.
Thank you extremely fine thank you.
Keep us in mind please keep us.
Please keep
Your submission in mind.
Entries so fine many fine
Winners selected not you.
Not you. Not quite
What we need
At this time not quite.
Keep in mind best of luck next time.
Editors wish you this guideline.
Best of selected regret.
Not chosen you were not able.
We inform our regret.
We reject your receive.
We receive we regret. Inform you we do.
We do as we do.
Today: To do: Don't forget.
Difficult choice we regret.
Space an issue weren't able. Limited
Space unable.
Please
Accept this issue.
Our complimentary
Gift to you.
Letterpressed gift in which you
Do not appear we regret you.
We regret to reject with respect
Please accept. Do

Not not accept
This reject
If you do
If you do
With respect
With respect
We reject you.

Frances McCue

Frances McCue is a writer and poet who serves as the writer-in-residence at the University of Washington's Undergraduate Honors Program. She was the founding director of Richard Hugo House from 1996 to 2006. McCue is a public scholar who brings community arts and culture projects together with work in the academy. McCue is the author of two poetry collections, *The Stenographer's Breakfast* and *The Bled*, a newly-released collection of poems about living in Morocco for a year. Her book on Richard Hugo, *The Car That Brought You Here Still Runs*, has been reviewed in newspapers throughout the Northwest and in national journals. She has been a Fulbright Senior Scholar, an Echoing Green Fellow and a Klingenstein Fellow.

Acknowledgments

"The Artifact" appears in *The Clear Cut Anthology*

The Architect's History

Into an elm so rotten
the flesh was soggy,
I slammed an ax.
When I pulled back
the blade, it squeaked.
I chopped squares
and the blocks
popped free.
For an afternoon
the sink and sing
held me and I made
steps up the tree.
My childhood,
clogged with the debris
of adult intentions,
fell into privacy.
I smoked cigars
or tobacco in bark
rolled like little leaf-
wrapped trees.
I'd test my lines
of sight to the creek
and tug the
smoke through me.

Now, I've become
the architect who
wants to flee this poem
she clamps me in.
Somehow, I end up
in conference rooms,
with flip charts and
wall mount TV's.
I imagine trees
and clocks and vistas.
Always: the sweet
squeak of my pencil

pulled away from
the print, and the arc
carved clear—
lovely and dead
things lifted by material.

The Artifact

Like cows, we gathered to the artifact.
Maybe we were bored.

The thing blew into our lives like a meteor.
Indeed, it looked like a thing torn

from space and tossed in a field. Only, it wasn't.
The thing was a chair.

"A chair?"
"Yes."

It is the simplest way to name
such an artifact, an ancestral wish,

a hand-me-down adrift—
How else to describe it?

This morning, it appeared
in the empty living room.

We do not know who placed it there,
but the designation said,

"This chair belongs to you."
We pulled up next to it.

We flicked aside our canes and walkers;
we cobbled our false teeth,

knicking them against our gums.
Click click natter natter.

"How does one actually sit on it?"
"Where do our legs go?" "Does it recline?"

The thing looked back at us,
holding its own secrets,

knowing and smug, about what it was
to be a chair. We circled it.

Now, as I tell it, I see that
our gathering was elegiac.

The twentieth century had passed
before us and we could not

understand the whole
expanse of it: the trite inventions,

unabashed cruelty—how it
sidewinded psychology to us,

instead of God. Our relic shone
like smeared tin with upholstery

pinned around the edges. We lumbered away,
in search of other furniture

more comfortable. Into our rooms,
we dispersed; we fled the chair.

It remains a thing, a place
where no one sits. It's of little use.

So when guests come, we recommend
the artifact. We say, "Be seated."

Of course we leave the room.
Best not to see a guest wrangle

with a chair that so easily outwits.
We're nearly blind and rickety

on our feet. We know better than to sit
in the thing. We wouldn't even dream of it.

In the Alley Sideways We Seek the Moon

This night
in the liddy lot of moon-not
There is a spell.

Moon, why not? She said.
Pointing to the space.

No orb, lunar wise.
Lid other-handed, she walked toward.

Little slippers, little whoosh
In the flitter-by
Hush. Light-dropping swords.

Aimee Nezhukumatathil

Aimee Nezhukumatathil is the author of *Miracle Fruit, At the Drive-In Volcano*, and most recently, *Lucky Fish*, all from Tupelo Press. Awards for her writing include the Pushcart Prize and an NEA Fellowship in Poetry. She is associate professor of English at SUNY-Fredonia. www.aimeenez.net

Acknowledgments

"Rain: A Catalog," "Kansas Animalia," and "The Secret of Soil" appear in *Lucky Fish* (Tupelo Press, 2011)

Rain: A Catalog

My son has not yet
found cause to hate

rain. Every plash
into a puddle forms

a plicata pattern
on my dress like

the iris edging
our yard in June.

It was once thought
if you want to make

it rain in India,
you need to beat

the shadow
of the Taj Mahal's

biggest finial
with your fist.

To this day, janitors
still find broken pieces

of bangles scattered
across the courtyard.

Kansas Animalia

I curtsy to the prairie turtle, running with all its might
to catch the paint line of a country road.
I pity the lone ostrich at the Wichita petting zoo,
who plucks out her own feathers because they sold
her mate to a place in Toledo. I cheer the prairie dog, who
keeps watch on the outskirts of his town, knows exactly
where to find a crunchy spider for dessert. Most of all,
I sing for the two-headed calf who managed to live
three whole days before it knelt beside its mama

and sank into the mud. Praise the mud and its confusion
with each quick slip of hoof. Praise the double song
of sadness from the sleep-sloppy mouths. Praise the farmer
who finally sussed it from the sludge and onto his back
while the mama kicked the farmer until he split open.
Praise his daughter who spied it all from her window.
Years later, she'll still have nightmares about that day.
The smell of linen and butter always bring her back.
Praise each groan and sigh from her fretful sleep.

The Secret of Soil

The secret of smoke is that it will fill
any space with walls, no matter
how delicate: lung cell, soapy bubble
blown from a bright red ring.

The secret of soil is that it is alive—
a step in the forest means
you are carried on the back
of a thousand bugs. The secret

I give you is on page forty-two
of my old encyclopedia set.
I cut out all the pictures of minerals
and gemstones. I could not take

their beauty, could not swallow
that such stones lived deep inside
the earth. I wanted to tape them
to my hands and wrists, I held

them to my thin brown neck.
I wanted my mouth to fill
with light, a rush of rind
and pepper. I can still taste it

like a dare across a railroad track,
sure with feet-solid step. I'm not
allowed to be alone with scissors.
I will always find a way to dig.

January Gill O’Neil

January Gill O'Neil is the author of *Underlife* (CavanKerry Press, 2009), her first poetry collection. She was featured in *Poets & Writers* magazine's January/February 2010 Inspiration issue as one of its 12 debut poets. A Cave Canem fellow, she is on the planning committee for the 2011 Massachusetts Poetry Festival, and lives with her two kids in Beverly, Massachusetts. She blogs at Poet Mom: www.poetmom.blogspot.com

In the Company of Women

for CM

Make me laugh over coffee,
make it a double, make it frothy
so it seethes in our delight.
Make my cup overflow
with your small happiness.
I want to hoot and snort and cackle and chuckle.
Let your laughter fill me like a bell.
Let me listen to your ringing and singing
as Billie Holiday croons above our heads.
Sorry, the blues are nowhere to be found.
Not tonight. Not here.
No makeup. No tears.
Only contours. Only curves.
Each sip takes back a pound,
each dry-roasted swirl takes our soul.
Can I have a refill, just one more?
Let the bitterness sink to the bottom of our lives.
Let us take this joy to go.

The Little Mermaid Walks Away

There's too much water in the ocean.
Each wave an echo, an unanswered wish
calling her to the surface. The pulsing current
through coral reefs means nothing to her
when the ocean's craggy floor
is pocked with the things
others throw away. She brushes her
cyclone of tangled hair with a fork.

How perfect does an apple taste?
A steak? A kiss? At night, she writes
her girlish notions against shafts of moonlight.
The morning hands them back.
There are no flaws in nature, so to walk
on pronged feet, to leave a footprint,
means walking out of a dream.
It means destroying a kingdom
only to build it again.

Body Politic

Praise our scars—
the small gashes
and the long,
serpentine tracks
that make up
our unbeauty.
Scar, from the
Greek word *eschara*,
meaning place of fire.
This is the body's politic,
reminding us that
the past existed.
Inside, what is tender
is retreaded by our living,
by wounds in the sidewalks
of dry skin. Never once
do we question
the sinkholes our bodies
drive into and repair
day after day.
No one but our
doctor or lover
can read the map
to our hurting.

Prayer

Tonight I pray to the god

of small children and broken toys.

Since it seems as though we are made

in Her image, thank you for the tiny curls

in my daughter's hair. Blessed is She

who holds those galactic swirls close to her beautiful head,

thanks for letting me run my fingers through them

as we read *Goodnight Moon* at the end of a long, wrecked day.

Thanks for her little hands with chipped nail polish

and the laughter ebbing from her coral lips.

God of the color pink, god of Dora the Explorer,

thank you for rain as we begin our journey into sleep,

let the sky fall one drop at a time.

That we can find ourselves

in this unearned sweetness,

to the god of small miracles

I say *Amen*.

Alicia Ostriker

Alicia Ostriker has published thirteen poetry collections, including *The Book of Seventy*, which received the 2009 National Jewish Book Award for Poetry. *The Crack in Everything* and *The Little Space: Poems Selected and New, 1969-1989*, were both National Book Award finalists. As a critic, Ostriker is the author of *Stealing the Language: The Emergence of Women's Poetry in America*, and other books on poetry and on the Bible. Ostriker teaches in the Low-Residency Poetry MFA Program of Drew University. www.rci.rutgers.edu/~ostriker/home.htm

Acknowledgments

"The Beautiful Morning Triptych" appears in *5 A.M.*
"Everywoman her Own Theology" appears in *The Imaginary Lover* (Univ. of Pittsburgh Press)
"Mastectomy" appears in *The Crack in Everything* (Univ. of Pittsburgh Press)

The Vow of The Old Woman, The Tulip, and The Dog

I must solve my life
said the old woman
thinking of her grandchildren
and of her marriage
and of her many former lovers

I must solve my life
said the red tulip, arranging her skirts
troubled by the ache of sunshine
the squirrels and dogs
far too hyperactive

I must solve my life, said the dog
torn between tame and wild
bouncing from chow bowl to street
addicted to human love
dumb animal

The Beautiful Morning Triptych

Oh what a beautiful morning
sang the old woman
striding past the tulip
without looking

Besame, besame mucho
sang the tulip
in a smooth yet throaty voice
like Cesaria Evora

Je ne regrette rien
sang the dog
cruising past the tulip
on his leash

Everywoman Her Own Theology

I am nailing them up to the cathedral door
Like Martin Luther. Actually, no,
I don't want to resemble that Schmutzkopf
(See Erik Erikson and N.O. Brown
On the Reformer's anal aberrations,
Not to mention his hatred of Jews and peasants),
So I am thumbtacking these ninety-five
Theses to the bulletin board in my kitchen.

My proposals, or should I say requirements,
Include at least one image of a god,
Virile, beard optional, one of a goddess,
Nubile, breast size approximating mine,
One divine baby, one lion, one lamb,
All nude as figs, all dancing wildly,
All shining. Reproducible
In marble, metal, in fact any material.

Ethically, I am looking for
An absolute endorsement of loving-kindness.
No loopholes except maybe mosquitoes.
Virtue and sin will henceforth be discouraged,
Along with suffering and martyrdom.
There will be no concept of infidels;
Consequently the faithful must entertain
Themselves some other way than killing infidels.

And so forth and so on. I understand
This piece of paper is going to be
Spattered with wine one night at a party
And covered over with newer pieces of paper.
That is how it goes with bulletin boards.
Nevertheless it will be there.
Like an invitation, like a chalk pentangle,
It will emanate certain occult vibrations.

If something sacred wants to swoop from the universe
Through a ceiling, and materialize,

Folding its silver wings,
In a kitchen, and bump its chest against mine,
My paper will tell this being where to find me.

Mastectomy
for Alison Estabrook

I shook your hand before I went.
Your nod was brief, your manner confident,
A ship's captain, and there I lay, a chart
Of the bay, no reefs, no shoals.
While I admired your boyish freckles,
Your soft green cotton gown with the oval neck,
The drug sent me away, like the unemployed.
I swam and supped with the fish, while you
Cut carefully in, I mean
I assume you were careful.
They say it took an hour or so.

I liked your freckled face, your honesty
That first visit, when I said
What's my odds on this biopsy
And you didn't mince words,
One out of four it's cancer.
The degree on your wall shrugged slightly.
Your cold window onto Amsterdam
Had seen everything, bums and operas.
A breast surgeon minces something other
Than language.
That's why I picked you to cut me.

Was I succulent? Was I juicy?
Flesh is grass, yet I dreamed you displayed me
In pleated paper like a candied fruit,
I thought you sliced me like green honeydew
Or like a pomegranate full of seeds
Tart as Persephone's those electric dots
That kept that girl in hell,
Those jelly pips that made her queen of death.
Doctor, you knifed, chopped and divided it
Like a watermelon's ruby flesh
Flushed a little, serious
About your line of work
Scooped up the risk in the ducts

Scooped up the ducts
Dug out the blubber,

Spooned if off and away, nipple and all.
Eliminated the odds, nipped out
Those almost insignificant cells that might
Or might not have lain dormant forever.

Nancy Pagh

Nancy Pagh has authored two award-winning collections of poetry, *No Sweeter Fat* (Autumn House Press book award) and *After* (Floating Bridge Press chapbook competition), and one book of nonfiction (*At Home Afloat*). Her work appears in numerous publications, including *Prairie Schooner, Crab Creek Review, Poetry Northwest, Rattle, The Bellingham Review*, and *O Magazine*. She was born in the island community of Anacortes, Washington, and currently teaches at Western Washington University.

Acknowledgments

"I Like to Be Still" and "Trying" appear in *After* (Floating Bridge Press, 2008)
"At the Erotic Bakery" appears in *Crab Creek Review*

At the Erotic Bakery

florid paper presses inside
the shop's front window
so no one can stand
on the street corner, nose to glass,
admiring the spectacular
phalluses that rise from royal icing
some white, some latte brown,
and for unclear reasons one purple
there, in the center of the cake case
attenuating an assortment of labia
cupcakes floating freestyle
through the arrangement, like pink
and apricot-tinted moths
now spent and opened
after a night's flight, draped
upon the small sweet mounds,
each diminutive and ornamented—
I thought somewhat regrettably—
with a single peanut M&M.

No cameras allowed.

We flit through the erotic bakery
because my friend's daughter wanted
a cookie, and my friend and I
we are not prudes, not us,
we do not titter nervously
about the Purple One
nor does the meticulous detail
of sugared glans escape our attention.

No cookies at the erotic bakery.

In the car driving home, Luxi asks
Mom, who buys those?
And we laugh. *Bridal showers,*
we tell her. *Bachelorette parties.*
And because I am not a parent
I add *high-school graduation,*
sweet sixteen, and

first communion as the tires
roll out the dark road beneath us
and the night-bugs frost the headlamps
and the Purple One rises again
in our soft imaginations.

Which is fine. Which is fine.
But let the erotic baker turn
on the woman he loves tonight,
the woman who moves like batter
who smells of ripe fruit and the extract of almonds
who flutters to his fingers
and gives away the recipe
for a filling he has never known,
never imitated in shortening, salt, or flour.

Kites

Some days all I think about is pancakes.

Heavy syrup. Carboholic.

I brush your hair, stroke your teeth with my tongue

like the smallest birds hitting windows.

I knew a horse in Albuquerque. Her rump.

Some kites fly without tails, some

like mice before the tractor's big rubber wheel.

Trying

after Marge Piercy

The people I love best are the ones who try: the aged who rise
early each damp morning and part the clump of coffee filters
with arthritic fingers—and the others who stay up
late after working all day in retail, hot pink curl of ear
pressing the receiver, listening to the friend who is selfish
but in agony now. I love the men who are fathers
to children, not buddies not video-game rivals not boys
themselves but clumsy men who ache over the fragility of sons,
but preserve the fragility of sons despite what everyone says.
I love those who feel no skill has come to them innate,
who will hold their small inland dogs again and again
above the sea on vacation, to watch in amazement
the knowing animal body that paddles through air. I love
the B+ student. The thick-chinned girl always picked
fourth when choosing sides for the softball team.
The lover who says it first. The lover who says it second
after a long, long pause. The lover who says it knowing
the answer is no, no, I am too broken. People who knit
things together. People willing to take things apart
and roll all the strands of yarn into new balls for next time.
The woman who loaded her backseat full of blankets and drove
for three days to the hurricane site. Even the loafer who tries
his mother's patience, who quietly speculates and eventually
decodes the universe for us all. Believe me, I have tried
to love others, the meager personalities who charm and butter,
the jaded the cynics the players and floaters all safe
in their cages, this life no responsibility they can own.
They see it too—how trying is always a risk,
a kind of vulnerability some choose for ourselves because
our fathers taught us well, our fathers taught us to try
to remain as fragile and full as this world that loves us.

I Like To Be Still
after Pablo Neruda

I like to be still: it is as though there never was
such a thing as waking, and crows beyond the window
are distant as the beaches with private hotels.
No one strips the bedding. No one sweeps the sand.

Everyone chooses not to touch some things.
And the soul of these things goes on dreaming
and seems far away like our own red birth.
I am like the word annunciation.

I like to be still in this room in the morning.
A sleeping cat pushes his back to my spine.
There is nothing to look forward to
so much as fondling his head and the sound he will make.

You misunderstand my silence. All things are my soul
and the quietest things are me most of all. This is true:
I am not entertaining in the way that you want.
My breasts never warranted an exclamation mark.

I like to be still: it is as though there never was
possibility then possibility taken away beyond windows
and stars and the high afternoon so remote like you
and everyone choosing to touch other things.

Alison Pelegrin

Alison Pelegrin is the author of three poetry collections, most recently *Big Muddy River of Stars* (2007) and *Hurricane Party* (2011), both from the University of Akron Press. The recipient of a creative writing fellowship from the National Endowment for the Arts, her poems have appeared in numerous print journals, and may also be found online at *Blackbird, Ploughshares, Poetry*, and *The Valparaiso Poetry Review.*

Acknowledgments

"Our Lady of Prompt Succor" appears in *Crab Orchard Review*
"Praying with Strangers" appears in *Copper Nickel*
"The Family Jewels" and "Hurricane Party" appear in
Barn Owl Review

The Family Jewels

Love me, love me not. I don't hate the South.
Or maybe I do. I hate fiction writers spewing
Faulkner's rules at me—*a writer without a bottle*
of whiskey is like a chicken without a goddamn head.
I learned that babysitting—snuck bourbon
in a Dixie cup then diluted the bottle down to rainwater
and compared my answers with theirs in a stack
of Playboy quizzes, vowing to catch up
by flashing a cab driver, answering the door naked.
Church of Faulkner fiction class in grad school,
we went back and forth: the museum's on fire
and it's up to you to choose between a Vermeer
and a random grandmother—you can only save one.
We all know what Faulkner said—*If a writer*
has to rob his mother, he will not hesitate.
'Ode on a Grecian Urn' is worth any number of old ladies.
I want to agree. As a poet I maybe should,
but I think of Emily Dickinson behind a screen
writing, all cameo and concentration, teaching,
I think, that it's the act, not artifact. I'm not in love
with Keats' Ode—'To Autumn' is better, but even *mists*
of mellow fruitfulness elicits a so what
when I think of my mother—a little old lady now,
with her netti pot and tissues up the sleeve. In her will
it says for me to pull the plug and bury her cheap,
instructions left in triplicate with Aunt Joan, the lawyer,
and in a box of rhinestones hog tied with bungee cords
and labeled, as a joke on thieves, The Family Jewels.

Hurricane Party

No way in hell the sky would do me wrong.
Even with the weatherman keening
in his yellow slicker, it just doesn't sink in.

Plywood, shrimp boots, sandbags, and booze.
Stuck in line at the hardware store,
pancakes for dinner after schools close early.
Before landfall, before the water comes
and anyone gets hurt,

it's always fun—
chanting the alphabet of past hurricanes
that never harmed besides a muck mosaic
in the streets,

the waterline's footprint
a jagged hem of leaves on the lawn.

Taping the windows, packing
for a midnight exodus, our map
the lava flow of headlights. In the car—
pillows, a coffee can for pee,
and *Michael, row the boat ashore.*

The aggravation makes the worst you've heard
seem not so bad, not even boating
from rooftop to rooftop after Betsy,

or cousin Chancy in the crook of a tree
delivered by a voice speaking out of the light:
Over here—dis child, he cold.

Is it chance, or is God listening when I beg
to be passed over, for someone to take my place
ripping up carpets and breathing the stench
of minnows shriveled on concrete?

Cameron Parish, Yucatan Peninsula,
the whole of Florida, Dominican Republic—
apologies for the times my blessings

have arrived at your expense—

a feast of outage-thawed seafood,
the easy work of peeling tape
from crossed-off windows,

each pane scraped clean
a day the calendar is giving back.

Praying with Strangers

Wish I could be funny again, like the old me,
    wild child with food and music on the mind,
        because I am worn out with bringing

nothing but needs to the hands of the Lord
    beginning that day I packed the kids in the car
        for a head start against The Hurricane.

Five hours north to the nearest hotel room,
    tears the whole way, like we knew what was coming,
        like we were going to be the ones prying apart

the automatic doors of the Winn Dixie
    to float out unfrozen frozen food.
        Oh Refugees, oh my stranded sisters

and brothers, we never looked away
    from the television set our campfire.
        We ate out until the money ran out,

then choked down charity—peanut butter,
    peanut butter, peanut butter, bread.
        I swam in the hotel pool, drawling

reminisces in the company of peers,
    anything to keep my head above water
        in the bible belt, where they don't sell beer

on Sundays. Bellyaching, praying with strangers—
    it became my life's work. Didn't want the job,
        but there I was, scratching out words, taking notes,

while my children, their foot soles filthy black,
    played rescue helicopter with their army people
        on the rooftop of the unmade bed.

Our Lady of Prompt Succor
Protect us from hurricanes and floods

Not Catholic but *almost,* my middle name
Marie iambic you. I knelt on rice
in Catholic schools, cropped the Our Father,
but you never wept tears of oil for me,
just stared off, disappointed, into space.
Mother Mary, in resin in our senior rings,
hitching a ride wherever our hands dared travel.
Oh, virginity!—a sin even to think it—me, Mary,
and a Brother Martin boy in the backseat
making our own weather—forecast fog,
and your tears the rain rising as steam from the streets.
They say your heart bleeds for the Crescent City,
in strange ways upending fate—the fire of 1812
miraculously snuffed at the convent steps,
dozens of hurricanes by your devoted prayed away.
Even when levees buckle and the rogue winds
devastate, your effigies remain mostly upright
in a thousand gardens, apparitions of lichens and white.
There are other hurricane saints, you know.
The gilded ones, Saint Hildegard of Hungary,
and Gregory the Wonderworker, not to mention
God's people on the ground: the Cajun boat brigade,
food looters, helicopter pilots, deputized nurses
sleeping in shifts in the hospital chapel.
You were there in the corner looking spent,
dusty silk flowers at your feet, like a beautified
Sister Hillary, our band camp chaperone. Has she
crossed over, her man shoes and mustache gone
to ash? Sister Mary Hillary up and down the hallway
with a flashlight, plagued by our boy talk,
her lullaby the Latin Mass. She prayed for us, you gave
your answer—infinity of pencil leads, the rain.

Susan Rich

Susan Rich is the author of three collections of poetry, *The Alchemist's Kitchen* (2010), *Cures Include Travel* (2006), and *The Cartographer's Tongue* (2000), which won the PEN West Award for Poetry. Her work has appeared in journals such as *The Antioch Review, Harvard Review*, and *Poetry International*. She has received awards from *The Times Literary Supplement*, Peace Corps Writers and the Fulbright Foundation. Before moving to Seattle, WA, Rich worked as a Peace Corps Volunteer in Niger, West Africa, an electoral supervisor in Bosnia, and a human rights educator in Palestine.
www.susanrich.net or visit her blog at:
www.thealchemistskitchen.blogspot.com

Acknowledgments

"Mohamud at the Mosque" appears in *Cures Include Travel* (White Pine Press, 2006)
"Letter to the End of the Year" appears in *The Alchemist's Kitchen* (White Pine Press, 2010)
"Andalusia" appears in *Pilgrimage: Story, Spirit, Witness, Place* V35

Andalusia

for Kimberly

Occasionally, we start from scratch.

A new roadway, a country, a woman
who commands us, *mirame.*

We travel roundabouts as if they might
teach us to negotiate

cloud caravans out of the city,

out of the rhythm of doorframes
accompanied by Lorca

postcards and *Nights at the Alhambra* tea.

~

I want to give you
syllables you can eat: tapas

of local tomatoes touched with ephemeral cheese;

oranges and lemon fruit
the size of scabby babies.

For you, I will silence the mourning doves

and offer the tilt-a-swirl of swifts
lifting up and out of the pepper tree.

And although I cannot gloss the language

of porn stars
for you, I'll purchase pink

flash cards of post-modern anatomy.

~

The night was cracked

and there were motionless salamanders;
the red signals of the Fiesta

lighting the windshield and the water

spray from your body ~

As you squatted before the A7, before the great tankards of gin,

and the world was yours
a quirk of moonlight in the queendom.

Mohamud at the Mosque
for my student upon his graduation

And some time later in the lingering
blaze of summer, in the first days
after September 11th you phoned—

if I don't tell anyone my name I'll
pass for an African American.
And suddenly, this seemed a sensible solution—

the best protection: to be a black man
born in America, more invisible than
Somali, Muslim, asylum seeker—

Others stayed away that first Friday
but your uncle insisted that you pray.
How fortunes change so swiftly

I hear you say. And as you parallel
park across from the Tukwila
mosque, a young woman cries out—

her fears unfurling beside your battered car
go back where you came from!
You stand, both of you, dazzling there

in the mid-day light, her pavement
facing off along your parking strip.
You tell me she is only trying

to protect her lawn, her trees,
her untended heart—already
alarmed by its directive.

And when the neighborhood
policeman appears, asks
you, asks her, asks all the others—

So what seems to be the problem?
He actually expects an answer,
as if any of us could name it—

as if perhaps your prayers
chanted as this cop stands guard
watching over your windshield

during the entire service
might hold back the world
we did not want to know.

Fragment To Be Considered Later

December, early morning

Remember the walk to the woodshed
at first light, after an hour spent with words.
Fix your mind on the blue bathhouse
quietly illuminated; the pump house still aglow.
Lift your chin to the pines, to the owl
call, even the moth on the porch wall.
You may do this. Lean into the window,
hold the cup of tea, the small sorrows.
Relax. The sky is open. Climb into it.
Even the snow.

Letter To The End Of The Year

Lately, I am capable of small things.

Peeling an orange.
Drawing a bath.
Throwing the cat's tinsel ball.

Believe me, this is not unhappiness.

Only one question ~
why this layering on of abeyance?

Though it is winter inside of me ~

there is also spring and fall.

Yellow tulips in need of planting
root in a basket by the door.

Tonight, mortality seems cloistered in a pinecone

close-windowed, remote.

What was the peak moment
of your happiness?

And how did you know?

For weeks, it's been oatmeal,
the Internet, an Irish shawl.

I realize, I am growing older
and stranger.

Please, don't misunderstand.

I am still impatient

still waiting for symbiant and swoon

the litter of blue-gold ~

a one-time constellation:

Now, before you go.

Rachel Rose

Rachel Rose has won awards for her poetry, her fiction, and her nonfiction. She has published poems, short stories and essays in Canada, the U.S., New Zealand and Japan, including *Poetry, The Malahat Review*, and *The Best American Poetry*. The author of two books, *Giving My Body to Science* and *Notes on Arrival and Departure*, she teaches at Simon Fraser University and is the founder of the "Cross-Border Pollination" reading series. www.rachelrose.ca

Waiting for the Biopsy Results

We don't talk about it. We put it out of mind.
It clings like mist, like cobweb, to our skin.
When I wake it presses, sticky, invisible,
and in that interlude I can't name the mood,
confuse the burst of anticipation with joy,
like waiting for a birth. Then the waiting names itself.
When the strange red poppy begins to bloom its fear
inside me, I refuse, I push back each petal to the hard
unbloomed green hat of the bud, the hat that women wear
when their hair falls out, I will not let it open its heart,
I will not take this flower until the call comes
and I must take this flower.

The Opposite of War

The opposite of war takes half an afternoon
costs seven dollars in parking
and does not solve the problem
we cannot solve. It is inconvenient
and stings a little.

It does only what it says it can do:
gives blood to strangers for a little more life,
a little more life. The opposite of war
has its arm on a table
with a tourniquet around it.
It goes on and on.
It looks away
from the thoughts of the man
who becomes a bomb.

The opposite of war comes down
to how the word *stranger*
is translated:
one blood sacrifice
or another.

Cherry trees create a spectacle, tossing their wet confetti
at the window. A child's hair falls out
on her pillow. Blood pools under the skin of the sky.
We're dizzy now. Our blue gift
flashes red at the exit. We don't speak to each other,
but we're lighter when we leave.
The opposite of war is not useless,
but nearly so. It bruises.
We get a cotton ball to staunch the flow.

Natasha Sajé

Natasha Sajé is the author of two books of poems, *Red Under the Skin* (Pittsburgh, 1994), and *Bend* (Tupelo Press, 2004), and many essays. Her work has been honored with the Robert Winner and Alice Fay di Castagnola Awards, a Fulbright fellowship, the Campbell Corner Poetry Prize, and the Utah Book Award. Sajé is a professor of English at Westminster College in Salt Lake City, and has been teaching in the Vermont College M.F.A. in Writing program since 1996.

Acknowledgments

"B" appears in *POOL*
"E" appears in *Prairie Schooner*
"S" appears in *Puerto del Sol*

B

Remember your fetal pig in high school, its veins and arteries pumped full of red and blue plastic, formaldehyde lingering under your fingernails? Bones: both the human body and the pig's contain 208, human extras usually lodged in the hand (phallanges) or the foot (tarsals), while porcine vertebrae can fuse to ribs, making counting difficult. Boar, whose flesh makes a delectable sauce for papardelle, whose long teeth could crunch a human hand but whose temper is kept in check rooting truffles under oak trees, and who are breeding again in the British countryside. Pigs make intelligent (and demanding) pets, although obesity can be a problem. My recipe for deviled ham would make you weep. Beelzebub=Lord of the Flies=Satan's right-hand-man=Demon of Gluttony. The Devil is often depicted with cloven feet. *The herd of swine and devils perished in the waters.* The sowe freten the child right in the cradel. A boar's dark bristles make an excellent hairbrush, picking up dust better than plastic, scratching the scalp the way the pig itself might enjoy its chin scratched. Francis Bacon wrote prose clean as bones. His descendant painted men to look like pigs.

E

essay, to try, from *exagiare,* to weigh out, examine

I was eleven and watching the Galloping Gourmet with his British-Australian accent and his glass of wine

learning how to get juice out of a lemon by rolling it hard on the counter

when the doorbell rang

my hair around cans to make it straight

the man next door, his receding hair combed back

erminea, the weasel whose fur turns from brown to white in winter

asked if anyone else were home

I said no

edentate, lacking teeth

asked if he could come in

electric, from Greek, *elektron*, amber, because it produces sparks when rubbed

I said no, I'm sorry

euphemism, to speak with good words

we stood   eye to eye

eutrophic: a body of water with so much mineral & organic matter
    the oxygen is reduced

until I slowly shut the door in his face

Eve, from Hebrew, living

pushing with both hands

Š

at the room of a sleeping child, a finger to the threshold

teeth drawn together
            hissing softened by lips
            echoed in the cave

                        little roof (strešica)

difference between a chocolatier (Kraš) and lime-
            stone (kras), white rocks
            struck by moon

as in sugar
which can be made from beets, cane, corn, maple, fruit, and milk

its sweetness rhymes with bees

we say one thing is not another thing
and in this language every letter is pronounced

cup gathering a drop of sound

            dusty taste of the water

            filmed skin after walking in the river

            sound the residue of letters

I'd like a letter that splinters

language from its parents to build
a house of sticks overlooking the sea, letting waves
instruct me—air
rushing through my teeth is also air
that could have passed through the tailpipe of a bus

I want happiness without a hole in it, the heroine says,
and the reader knows she's doomed to a life of fissures

subterranean, so deep you can live in them, deeper than the highest
mountains are high, stalactites forming overhead
gypsum flowers like wallpaper

in such darkness the pale pink
olm, his degenerated eyes covered
by skin, can live to a hundred
wan cousin of the newt or salamander
finds his way via smell

even Proteus, shepherd of the sea's flocks, cannot
protect him from polluted groundwater
and his own rarity

he lives only in one place on earth
a place where š is uttered

and might, if things were different, be
a dragon in the ocean's waving

fricative, or at least a snake with a crown

none poisonous in this quiet country

Slovenia

Peggy Shumaker

Peggy Shumaker is Alaska State Writer Laureate. Her most recent book of poems is *Gnawed Bones*. Her lyrical memoir is *Just Breathe Normally*. The poems in this anthology come from an Eco-Arts writing workshop in Costa Rica. Professor emerita from University of Alaska Fairbanks, she teaches in the Rainier Writing Workshop and at many conferences and festivals.
www.peggyshumaker.com

Basilisk Lizard
for Bill Kloefkorn

Lusty jitterbug
amplified by
corrugated rust

scares the bejejus
out of us. Before
roof flakes

settle, freckle
rust-earth
tiles, you skitter

toward water. Your toes
hinge over, longer
than your feet.

Little king, named
for a made-up
mess, part rooster,

part dragon, part
snake, you're very much awake
cooling your tail in the pool,

lifting, alert,
to every footfall,
wingbeat, breath.

With a single glance,
the story goes,
the basilisk

could stop
a heart. One step
too close

and you're
panic incarnate—

Jesus Christ

Lizard zipping
zigzag on hind legs,
kicking up

trails of rain,
salvation's sip sip
sip into mist.

Venom

The gardener
bashes in

the gorgeous
triangular head

of the fer-de-lance,
most venomous

víbora he knows.
Ay! One bite

and you're dead.
His forked stick

lifts looped
lank snake,

draped away
from his legs.

I ask to look—
slithers to earth

spoiled coil
turned clay.

Hermosa, I sigh.
Mosaic

scales, cream,
black, brown.

He nods.
Hermosa y

peligrosa. Muy
peligrosa.

Our guide

conjures prayers,

apologies.
The forked stick

slings pure danger
behind the shed.

Anhinga Drying Her Wings

Purely practical, we know,
her need to hold herself open

to let what sun she can catch
ease the river from her wings.

And yet. And yet.

Martha Silano

Martha Silano's books are *Blue Positive* (Steel Toe Books 2006), *What the Truth Tastes Like* (Nightshade Press 1999), and *The Little Office of the Immaculate Conception* (Saturnalia 2011). Her poems have appeared in *American Poetry Review, TriQuarterly, AGNI, The Best American Poetry 2009*, and elsewhere. Martha has been awarded grants and fellowships from Washington State Artist Trust, Seattle 4-Culture, the Arizona Poetry Center, and the Millay Colony for the Arts, among others. She teaches at Bellevue College and blogs at www.bluepositive.blogspot.com

Acknowledgments

"What I Will Tell the Aliens," "Others," "Ode to Imagination," and "It's All Gravy" appear in *The Little Office of the Immaculate Conception* (Saturnalia Books, 2011)

It's All Gravy

a gravy with little brown specks
a gravy from the juices in a pan

the pan you could have dumped in the sink
now a carnival of flavor waiting to be scraped

loosened with splashes of milk of water of wine
let it cook let it thicken let it be spooned or poured

over bird over bovine over swine
the gravy of the cosmos bubbling

beside the resting now lifted to the table
gravy like an ongoing conversation

Uncle Benny's pork-pie hat
a child's peculiar way of saying *emergency*

seamlessly   with sides of potato of carrot of corn
seamlessly   while each door handle sings its own song

while giant cicadas ricochet off cycads and jellyfish sting
a gravy like the ether they swore the planets swam through

luminiferous   millions of times less dense than air
ubiquitous   impossible to define   a gravy like the God

Newton paid respect to when he argued
that to keep it all in balance to keep it from collapsing

to keep all the stars and planets from colliding
sometimes He had to intervene

a benevolent meddling like the hand
that stirs and stirs as the liquid steams

obvious and simple   everything and nothing
my gravy your gravy our gravy   the cosmological constant's

glutinous gravy   an iridescent and variably pulsing gravy the gravy of implosion   a dying-that-births-dueodenoms gravy

gravy of doulas of dictionaries and of gold
the hand stirs   the liquid steams

and we heap the groaning platter with glistening
the celestial chef looking on as we lift our plates

lick them like a cat come back from a heavenly spin
because there is oxygen in our blood

because there is calcium in our bones
because all of us were cooked

in the gleaming Viking range
of the stars

Others

1. Pancake

We like our batter fluffy, so we sift.
Whole-wheat vs. white? So Pre-Big Bang.
There's an aura all around us,
yet nobody flips.

2. Sombrero

It might be a lot to get your head around,
but the black hole inside this crown is a billion times
the mass of your sun. Large as we are, we admire
your string of campfires guiding the departed toward Valhalla.

3. Exclamation Point

It's true! We're elongated! A rectangle aimed NW
at Mag 9! Aka the dot! With pulses of nebulosity!
Worth your time to find!

4. Taffy

There's a bridge between two of us resembling
those stretching bands of sticky goo
from deepest Jersey. Fralinger's famous—

Peach, Strawberry, Molasses Mint.
Craps schmaps. We prefer it here, pulling
and snapping while you lose your shirt playing slots.

5. Apple Core

Dim and distant—900 light years from where you hail,
we pride ourselves on heirlooms—Liberty, Spartan, Pink Pearl.
Winesaps and Wickson Crabs. Your biggest mistake? Letting
the Arkansas Beauty and the Tuscaloosa disappear.
This one? Gnawed on by a giant blue mouth,
then tossed out here, the farthest star in what
your kind call Cygnus.

6. Hamburger

Just be glad you're good and far away,
cuz the shit going down in this burg
makes your Agnes and Ike look like sun showers.
What happened first was a giant collision—imagine
a bacon and cheese slamming into a Coney.
The bacon went flying, while the mustard,
super-heated, shot out the opposite ends
at the speed of light. So now our bun's
got these spinning, spewing, fiery jets.
It's a mess! Not enough napkins to clean it up,
and no order of Mountain Dew to douse it.

7. Vacuum Cleaner

55 million light years away and receding briskly
from your dirty carpets and floors. Sometimes
it feels we were put here to mock you—us
and the folks who live in the Maytag. Cleaning,
and the loathing of it: maybe it's the true leveler,
our common ground. Let's strike a deal: we'll stop
the guilt-tripping if you stop sending spaceships
to places you don't need to go. Spend your money
cleaning up your own galaxy! (How's that
for a bunch of hot air?)

8. Tarantula

I know these guys give you the creeps,
but most of their sting is myth (no worse
than a bee's). Ours towers the ones that scuttle up
your Escalante Staircase. Good thing we're far
from your peeling front door, or else
we'd be casting shadows all over
your milky-white ass.

9. Footprint

That's right, a genuine I-was-here.
Judging by your passion for carving graffiti

into aspens, for re-reruns of *Planet of the Apes*,
you'd fit right in.

10. Dark Doodad

A long brown ribbon of doo-hickey,
like the ribbon of tongue hanging
from your don't-know-doodly-squat
mouth. If you've come here expecting
reassurances, you're in the wrong place.
Here we teach graveyard. Here our favorite language
is the one most dead.

What I Will Tell the Aliens

I will tell them about our clapping,
our odometers, and our skillets.

I will take them to a place of fierce
lightning, to a place of tombstones

and of gridlock, and I will tell them
of geckos, of ecstatic moments,

all about our tchotchkes, our temples,
our granite-countered kitchens.

Give me an alien and I will give it
a story of unfathomable odds,

of erections and looting. Show me
an alien and I will show it the sorrows

of the centuries, all wrapped up
in a kerchief, all wrapped up

in a grandmother's black wool coat.
Bring me an alien right now,

and I will show it the misery
of stilettos, of pounding out

tortillas and gyros. Please—
send me an alien, and I will give it

a bloody nose, and then I will show it a great
humanitarian gesture, 10,000 tents

when 600,000 are needed. Let me
talk to these aliens about shoe-shiners

and rapture, of holidays and faxes;
let me pray with the aliens for the ice

to stop melting, for the growths to stop
growing, for a gleam to remain on our lips

long after the last greasy French fry is gone.

Ode to Imagination

and image, Vostok 1 hurling Yuri Gagarin
200 miles above us, what the optic nerve's

efforant fibers unstitch, then carry its post-
orbit parachuting news to the retina. News

the earth is blue, so we look and when we do
our brain's not calling up a replica from its cache

of Polaroids stuffed in an attic drawer,
but a brand new view of vortex, tundra, crashed,

of John Glenn's capsule, with John Glenn inside!
At the point of re-entry, his tin-can home sustaining

quadruple-digit temps. How are you imagining it?
I'm seeing half a dozen loafered, skinny-tied guys

cozied around a computer the size of the Gorge
in George, Glenn, squeezed in, bolted-up, triple-checking

Friendship's gauges. Fragile, fragile like an eggshell,
a cool, crisp morning in August. And Glenn,

not much good at like or as, with no small steps
or giant leaps up his space-suited sleeve the sky

in space is very black. This moment of twilight
is very beautiful . . . Okay, so we can't all be Keats,

and besides, could a scop have stood the stress of a strap
from the retropackage swinging around, fluttering

past the capsule window? Would you've preferred
the poet-astronaut spurting metaphors as the smoking

apparatus ignites? Glenn kept his white-knuckled wits,
and the rest is Apollo 11, the ghost drum ungoblined,

the silent victory trumpet triumphant, a halo go round
the moon. But back to image, the flash in the dark,

back to the viewer taking it in Mama, wanna see,
wanna see? Mama, you're not looking! Mama lifting off

in her Cosmodrome, to a place where image meets
interference, life by a thousand shadows, the interplay

between brain and eye working overtime
to lift us off this earth.

Judith Skillman

Judith Skillman is the author of twelve collections of poetry, most recently *The White Cypress* (Cervéna Barva Press, 2011). She is the recipient of grants from Washington State Arts Commission, Academy of American Poets, and other organizations. Her poems have appeared in *Prairie Schooner, Midwest Quarterly, The Iowa Review, New Poets of the American West*, and many other journals and anthologies. Skillman has an M.A. in English Literature from the University of Maryland. She is a writer, educator, and editor. See www.judithskillman.com

Acknowledgments

"Epstein Barr" appears in *Journal of the American Medical Association (JAMA), Poetry and Medicine Column*, 2009
"October" appears in *Hawaii Pacific Review*

October

And the wild rose
blooms again in stillness before rain.
October, song of my sister, of the psalms
said for gratitude against the coming

of sickness and gray days—one long day
lasts the whole of winter, one long night
that never lightens.
The wild rose strains to birth

one more blossom, to tinge the edge
of winter's sword with blood.
We who live in houses—
the lucky ones, we see and do not understand

men who sleep beneath bridges,
their heads cradled in cardboard boxes.
We know the tides come and go
as sickness comes and goes.

Our neighbor's bones will break and mend,
our children's children will fall
and be well. October, and the wild rose
raises itself up

at once plain and pretty
as if to right every wrong
done to the kingdom of ants and bees—
all those who live communally.

Epstein Barr

At the bottom
of the tea cup,
the last leaves of lemon grass
spell a new fortune:
There will be a nap in your future.

That future has already
become
a past. Each day's worth
of tea-leavings:
a bog
from which my tired body,
mired
hip-to-shoulder—
tries to slog its slow way
way up from.

In the kitchen, the bright
clatter of cutlery. And
the high-pitched chatter,
the laughter
of relatives
I'm named after.

Their sharpened knives
chop chives on the oiled
block. Heady scents
rise from
wooden scars.

It will be gradual,
the return to health—
tendered by the same
hidden hands
that furrow my brow,
give me my
upside-down smile.

I am the joke

my family of strangers visits.
I am their laughter
and sigh,
their catharsis at not being me
palpable
as a lemon

stung by its second cut.

Becalmed

The cherry in flower,
the children gone,
the lust for lust
grown into a different creature,
one who sits in a patch of sun.

The sky-ships
welded together like clouds
nibbled at the edge
by portraiture's downy curls
and the blue gaze of youth.

A willow gestures, hemmed
by the same kite strings
that bind a woman to the hours.
Her figure changed by what
she cannot resist—

that pear listing
on the sill, this apple pressed
against another apple
in a crystal bowl.
Whatever the wind possessed,

it released to wander
over these lands changed
from exotic to familiar,
a sleight of hand
turning courtyard to yard,

the fountain at the center
of the square holding nymphs
and cherubs above water
as if both were innocent.
The cherry squanders its beauty

in bursts, ousts its scent
like a provocateur—
coyness overflowing the bowl
where child and woman
lived for years under the same roof.

Patricia Smith

Patricia Smith's six books of poetry include *Blood Dazzler*, a finalist for the 2008 National Book Award, and one of NPR's top five books of 2008, and *Teahouse of the Almighty*, a National Poetry Series selection. *Shoulda Been Jimi Savannah* will be released in spring 2012. Her work has appeared in *Poetry, The Paris Review, TriQuarterly* and in both *Best American Poetry* and *Best American Essays 2011*. She is a professor at the CUNY/College of Staten Island.

Acknowledgments

"The Reemergence of the Noose" appears in *Asheville Poetry Review*
"Eyewitness News" appears in *The Drunken Boat*
"Baby Born Holding Heart in Hand" appears in *The Cortland Review*

Eyewitness News
Soweto, Johannesburg South Africa, April 1994

The gritty film that CNN will treasure
will show her this way:

A mother, her glazed and bulging eyes
locked in the shimmer that creeps toward weeping,
pudgy body easing into metronome,
the boom and click of her tight new dress shoes
giving the bored choir a texture to climb.

Thank God, she's not a howler.

This will please the masses
who click their remotes,
pass the Diet Pepsi
and receive her into their homes over dinners
of sticky rice and saucy chunks of meat.
Neatly boxed and calmly hued, she is dignity byte,
incapable of ruining the family hour
by baring her teeth and demanding what she has lost.

But here, propped sweaty in this tiny church,
we wheeze in the musk of closeness and death,
swat away the gorged and sluggish flies
who gossip buzz, whisper on our skin with spindly legs,
dance wildly on the dead boy's nose.

He was 13, grace turning his back
to the bomb just before the blast.
Beneath the thin sheet that covers the place
where his legs should be,
there is the rustle
of nothing.
Damn those tattered gym shoes and pants legs,
stuffed with paper and sticks.

But his torso is memory, the fuel of mothers.
Ignore the singed eyebrow,
the missing cheek,
the doomed fly buzzing in the tight crown of hair,

the half-arm,
his mother's blistered focus.

And the camera, in its sugared edit,
ignores the procession, her sudden unhinging.
As the casket is closed by six identical boys
in wing-hemmed shirts, the mother's body stiffens,
bucks, crashes into the pew,
fists splinter the dry wood, hands roar and flail,
paperback Bibles fly, her mouth opens
wide and soundless upon raw teeth.
Head twists until neck wails and she is carried,
a squirming X,
a woman at each hand,
a man at each foot,
one dry breast popped loose,
already a shoe gone.

Already a shoe gone. Already a foot gone. A leg.
Already a leg gone. Two legs. A life.
Already her son gone, the moon following.
Try stuffing her hollow heart with paper,

paper and sticks.

The Reemergence Of The Noose

Some lamp sputters its dusty light across some
desk. Some hand, in a fever, works the fraying
brown hemp, twisting and knifing, weaving, tugging
tight this bellowing circle. Randy Travis
on the radio, steamy twangs and hiccups,
blue notes backing the ritual of drooping
loop. Sweat drips in an awkward hallelujah.
God glares down, but the artist doesn't waver—
wrists click rhythm, and rope becomes a path to
what makes saviors. The loop bemoans its need to
squeeze, its craving for a breath within the ring.

Baby Born Holding Heart In Hand
Raipur, India, November 2005

Imagine holding it there, thrumming, taunt,
unbridled crave in an unfinished fist,
not caring it's the reason she exists
at least for this moment. But watch it haunt
the gone dreams of all who see it throbbing,
soft pulsing, blood metronome, raw engine
drumming her death into maybe, robbing
us of what we need to believe. Again.

One doctor feels God's presence, one does not
(chilled, he eyes the trash). A nurse wants to snatch
the beating thing, hold it to her chest, and match
heartbeats. She thinks *Maybe I ought*
to pray. The child, with life to overcome,
dimmed by their indecision, shields the drum.

For Jermaine, Six, Dead In Boston

Spent bullets sparkle on streets grimy with the thud of winter.

Knives bulge odd angles in children's pockets, and any one
of their upturned words could bring us another you.
Promising harmony, Christmas carols blare twisted lyric
from behind doors wedged tight.
You do not stop being dead.

Thought it would never be again, but here's tomorrow,
a snippet of unturned year, no blood spraying its pure slate,
no tiny wreckage splayed there.

A storefront Santa, yellowing beard askew,
one exposed cheek gin-swollen, still asks his starlit questions.
Not far from his feet, the chalk outline of your body
waits like a slap under the snow for spring to return.

Ann Spiers

Ann Spiers' poems appear in many journals and anthologies. She holds an MA in Literature and Creative Writing from the University of Washington. She leads writing seminars and workshops in diverse venues such as colleges, poetry festivals, environmental centers, and poet-in-the-schools programs. Her chapbooks include *Long Climb into Grace* (FootHills Publishing, "Poets on Peace Series"), *The Herodotus Poems* (Brooding Heron Press), *Volcano Blue, Tide Turn*, and *The Wild Taste*, fine-press collaborations with Catherine Michaelis of May Day Press. Ann is a fifteen-year member of a writers' group. www.annspiers.com

Copalis Crossing

i
The banana bread is done
when she inserts a straw
into its risen dome
and the gesture brings back
all the times
she yanked the straw
out of the kitchen broom
punctured the crust
and loved the clean pullout
    him and the warm bread
    gone

ii
At the table
he tugs
a fist full of seeds
out of the pumpkin

She stands in the door jamb
and watches rain
    fill the ditches
    and now fills
    the road's long ruts
this is how
autumn slips away
and how again the rain
    keeps them inside
    alone

iii
He says
something about the moon
rounding for winter
he watches her posed there
looking into the night
ready to close the door

Right then
how her skin glows

makes him think
    of light flowing off
    the great heron's wings
he opens his mouth
the image that lifted
    him closer to her
    gone

Street Fighting, Bangkok

Under the Rama V on-ramp,
toads with fat bellies leap
through no-man's-land.
We photograph a headless Buddha,
his shrine nailed to a utility pole.
Orange peels fill his plastic alms bowl.
Helicopters overhead, low, rumbly.
Children stop playing hide and seek.

In the morning market, pig organs hang:
liver, heart, testicles, tongue.
From a shoe stall, I buy three pairs
of fancy slip-ins, cloth and brittle glue.
Children squat and play in a tight circle.
A centipede, like a whacky zipper, courses
across the sidewalk. The kids see it coming,
rise and skip backwards, away.

At the boulevard's end, skyscrapers
line up. Plate glass windows
protect real shoes and Vuitton totes.
In the square, the Red Shirts camp within
sharpened bamboo and smoking tires.

Stopping, we commandeer blue plastic
chairs, soft with sun. We buy coffee.
We watch on the street TV
the Red Shirts who, a block over, hoist
white plastic chairs against sniper fire.
In the noise, a Red Cross worker
distributes free fortune cookies,
individually wrapped, her soles sticky
with fish sauce and blood.

At the wat's entry, we kill time
as the kids teach us how to remove
our flipflops without breaking gait.

A.E. Stallings

A. E. Stallings is an American poet who has lived in Athens, Greece since 1999. She has published two collections, *Archaic Smile* and *Hapax*, and a verse translation of *Lucretius, The Nature of Things* (Penguin). A new collection of poems is forthcoming from Northwestern University Press.

Acknowledgments

"The Catch" and "The Mother's Loathing of Balloons" appear in *Poetry Magazine*
"Ultrasound" appears in 32 *Poems; Hapax* (TriQuarterly/Northwestern University Press)
"First Love: A Quiz" appears in *The Nebraska Review; Hapax* (TriQuarterly/Northwestern University Press)

First Love, A Quiz

He came up to me:

a) in his souped-up Camaro
b) to talk to my skinny best friend
c) and bumped my glass of wine so I wore the ferrous stain on my sleeve
d) from the ground, in a lead chariot drawn by a team of stallions black as crude oil and breathing sulfur; at his heart, he sported a tiny golden arrow

He offered me:

a) a ride
b) dinner and a movie, with a wink at the cliché
c) an excuse not to go back alone to the apartment with its sink of dirty knives
d) a narcissus with a hundred dazzling petals that breathed a sweetness as cloying as decay

I went with him because:

a) even his friends told me to beware
b) I had nothing to lose except my virginity
c) he placed his hand in the small of my back and I felt the tread of honey bees
d) he was my uncle, the one who lived in the half-finished basement, and he took me by the hair

The place he took me to:

a) was dark as my shut eyes
b) and where I ate bitter seed and became ripe
c) and from which my mother would never take me wholly back, though she wept and walked the earth and made the bearded ears of barley wither on their stalks and the blasted flowers drop from their sepals
d) is called by some men hell and others love
e) all of the above

Ultrasound

What butterfly—
Brain, soul, or both—
Unfurls here, pallid
As a moth?

(Listen, here's
Another ticker,
Counting under
Mine, and quicker.)

In this cave
What flickers fall,
Adumbrated
On the wall?—

Spine like beads
Strung on a wire,
Abacus
Of our desire,

Moon-face where
Two shadows rhyme,
Two moving hands
That tell the time.

I am the room
The future owns,
The darkness where
It grows its bones.

The Catch

Something has come between us—
It will not sleep.
Every night it rises like a fish
Out of the deep.

It cries out with a human voice,
It aches to be fed.
Every night we heave it weeping
Into our bed,

With its heavy head lolled back,
Its limbs hanging down,
Like a mer-creature fetched up
From the weeds of the drowned.

Damp in the tidal dark, it whimpers,
Tossing the cover,
Separating husband from wife,
Lover from lover.

It settles in the interstice,
It spreads out its arms,
While its cool underwater face
Sharpens and warms:

This is the third thing that makes
Father and mother,
The fierce love of our fashioning
That will have no brother.

The Mother's Loathing of Balloons

I hate you,
How the children plead
At first sight—

I want, I need,
I hate how nearly
Always I

At first say *no*,
And then comply.
(Soon, soon

They will grow bored
Clutching *your*
Umbilical cord)—

Over the moon,
Lighter-than-air,
Should you come home,

They'd cease to care—
Who tugs you through
The front door

On a leash, won't want you
Anymore
And will forget you

On the ceiling—
Admittedly,
A giddy feeling—

Later to find you,
Puckered, small,
Crouching low

Against the wall.
O thin-of-skin
And fit to burst,

You break for her
Who wants you worst.
Your forebear was

The sack of the winds,
The boon that gives
And then rescinds,

Containing nothing
But the force
That blows everyone

Off course.
Once possessed,
Your one chore done,

You float like happiness
To the sun,
Untethered afternoon,

Unkind,
Marooning all
You've left behind:

Their tinfoil tears,
Their plastic cries,
Their wheedling

And moot goodbyes,
You shrug them off—
You do not heed—

O loose bloom
With no root
No seed.

Joannie Kervran Stangeland

Joannie Kervran Stangeland's work has most recently appeared in *Crab Creek Review, Iota, San Pedro River Review, Valparaiso Poetry Review*, and *Painted Bride Quarterly*. Joannie is also the author of two poetry chapbooks, and she has been a Jack Straw Writer and has taught classes at Richard Hugo House.

Following Picasso

I have traveled through my rose period,
sun coloring clouds, blushing the air
even through cold glass. Winter softened
in those hours—then delicate,
the bare trees fine lace against a sky

that drifted from pink, pale coral
to blue, and how I moved
into my own corners of cerulean,
the lapis afternoons, hues
of slate, of water running under snow,

a somber gray shading the dull day
dragging to the deeper cobalt
cloak of night—my eyes blue
with evening, my skin blue from waiting,
my dreams doused in blue.

So heavy the shade, I tried to strip it off
like a cotton shirt from your shoulders,
like a leaf from an artichoke.
Each cunning layer, a little pointed,
hurt when I pulled it—

I wanted to see every face
at once, to open and lay plain
the trees inside the trees,
the lace inside your rose,
the eyes inside your sky.

The Crows' Song

Sing bone and scrap,
twig and old silk,
twine and foil,
sing oil and rain.
Bring evening and sing
to the sky as it falls
in blue and then lavender,
gray and then night.
Sing bright when the first light
sharpens the rooftops
and trees, when water
glistens on grass
and the lake lays out
flat as an eye.

They told us we had
no voice, no song,
and yet we wheel, we fly,
a swarm of black wings
flinging the dusk.
We sing of beak and claw,
of scavenger trash. We sing
and we welcome the dawn
before anyone.

The Fledgling

Wings rush past, a feather from touching,
quick wind as they swish by seconds after
I see the fledgling hunched against the ground.

The caws rain down faster, louder.
I think of hard beaks, this murder
bent on protection.

My arms remember the small weight
of my son, fragile—breathing, sucking,
finding his thumbs, legs, language.

He left the nest and comes back,
testing the world and his own wings.
I watch and cannot chase away

marauders, can't shield him
his own shadow that tags behind
like a black feather carried on a gust.

I stride as fast as I can, not knowing
how far I must walk
before the crows trust I am no trouble.

And how beautiful,
this young bird. We love
our babies fiercely, or we eat them.

Marilyn L. Taylor

Marilyn L. Taylor is the author of six collections of poetry, the most recent of which, *Going Wrong*, was published in 2009 by Parallel Press. Her award-winning work has also appeared in many anthologies and journals, including *The American Scholar, Poetry, Valparaiso Review, Measure, Mezzo Cammin, Able Muse,* and *The Raintown Review*. She taught poetry and poetics at the University of Wisconsin-Milwaukee for many years, and is currently a Contributing Editor for *The Writer* magazine, where her columns on craft appear bimonthly. Marilyn served as Poet Laureate of Wisconsin for 2009 and 2010. www.mlt-poet.com

Acknowledgments

"The Blue Water Buffalo" appears in *The Emily Dickinson Awards Anthology*, 2005 (Universities West Press)
"Reading the Obituaries" appears in *The Formalist*

The Blue Water Buffalo

One in 250 Cambodians, or 40,000 people,
have lost a limb to a landmine.
~*Newsfront*, U.N. Development Programme Communications Office

On both sides of the screaming highway, the world
is made of emerald silk—sumptuous bolts of it,
stitched by threads of water into cushions
that shimmer and float on the Mekong's munificent glut.

In between them plods the ancient buffalo—dark blue
in the steamy distance, and legless
where the surface of the ditch dissects
the body from its waterlogged supports below

or it might be a woman, up to her thighs
in the lukewarm ooze, bending at the waist
with the plain grace of habit, delving for weeds
in water that receives her wrist and forearm

as she feels for the alien stalk, the foreign blade
beneath that greenest of green coverlets
where brittle pods in their corroding skins
now shift, waiting to salt the fields with horror.

Reading the Obituaries

Now the Barbaras have begun to die,
trailing their older sisters to the grave,
the Helens, Margies, Nans—who said goodbye
just days ago, it seems, taking their leave
a step or two behind the hooded girls
who bloomed and withered with the century—
the Dorotheas, Eleanors and Pearls
now swaying on the edge of memory.
Soon, soon, the scythe will sweep for Jeanne
and Angela, Patricia and Diane—
pause, and return for Karen and Christine
while Susan spends a sleepless night again.
  Ah, Debra, how can you be growing old?
  Jennifer, Michelle, your hands are cold.

Molly Tenenbaum

Molly Tenenbaum is the author of the forthcoming *The Cupboard Artist* (Floating Bridge Press, 2011), *Now* (Bear Star Press, 2007), and *By a Thread* (Van West & Co, 2000). Honors include a 2007 residency at Hedgebrook, participation in the 2007 Jack Straw Writers Program, and a 2009 Washington State Artist Trust Fellowship. She plays Appalachian stringband music and has two CDs: *Instead of a Pony* and *Goose and Gander*. She teaches English at North Seattle Community College, and gives music lessons at home in Seattle. www.mollytenenbaum.com

Acknowledgments

"My Eyebrows" appears in *Crab Creek Review*

My Eyebrows

Once, a three-hundred-pound man with spitty fat lips
said "Never pluck them."
I've brushed them with red ink
and pressed them on paper.
I believe they're better in blue.
I've lipsticked and sealed them
on letters, a kiss. Need negatives
to un-mirror the prints. I'll toss them
on fabric, stitch bristling skirts,
and when I raise my hem. . .

Here, take my arch business card.
In the park, I've wired a controller, remote,
and zoomed them inches from your egg salad.
Hey, race your kite.

They've been tatting and grandmothers,
foxtails and muffins. Been mistletoe.
They've been an old car, throwing oil.
When they are sad, they are bumpkins
itching with straw, when happy,
rabbits in lettuce. Sometimes they scurry
belowbanks to hide from coyotes.

Now, their names are Ginger and Pickles,
and one laps haddock while the other topples the biscuit tin.
In their shop they sell boomerangs and springboards.
In summer, they give free bouquets.
In winter, they close, but you can come in.
Swing the door to set off peal after peal of bells.

The Pillows

The pillows, they breathe out and in, bedroom air
of fly-wing, bedroom air of gnat leg, flea dirt.

Take them in, the little tickles, pour them out, a speckled song.

Mom's hair and skin, scribbles and flakes,
cocklebur through the white case to the thin inner cover, foxtail
even through that to the foam—

my mother's wisps, her grease-dust, her drawing brows,
her *Oh!* with eyebrows up, her pine-motes, her white pith,
her parchment, her maple-wings,
her thousand hummingbirds in a thousand flowers
all sinking in the pillow's sling
like blood when the heart stops,
back body purpling, front body pale.

Or at the bottom of the birdhouse, a titmouse makes her nest.

Or gravity gathers them to the middle, the bits of my mother,
a small heart in foam.

Or like the fifty trillion neutrinos that pass through the body
every second, her cells through the sheet, mattress, floorboards,
her cells through the crawlspace and possums.

Her cut-up pins, her crushed leaves,
her shavings of wax,
the pillow's cross-section
a pencil sketch, Studies in Seeds,
pods whole, pods from top and each side,
and pods burst, shooting fuzz-spangled dots.

Open-weave body, singing body.

Someone should lift me and squint at me, give a fluff
and plop me, fat drop slapping water, my head
in the middle and air swirling up till I sleep there,
my sighs and flutters, my whiffles and trills.

The Rose Daughter

Mom and Dad can't help when she blooms like a fry pan's crazy oil,
blooming scarves that don't stop, blooming dumplings in syrup, blooming
dream-birds in all sizes every which way.

Who to call, what kind of doctor.

Too much apricot, too much maroon,
she hides in her room, her music, red mist through the door,
the dew pink soaking their passing slippers, wicking wet
auroras up their bathrobe hems.

In green sleeves longer than her hands,
she can't eat, can't lean on the table for thorns.
Can't even talk, fog of forget-me-nots at her feet,
her thousand petals crammed, her stamens
with ruffles like petals, her petals
with stamen-hairs waving alive at the edges.

They're always asking her worst question—
what to be when she grows up. Just look
at her navel of sparklers, her tongues
that gutter and spout, tongues that turn all the way over.
Strewing herself before herself, where she walks, it hurts.
Folding her hands, folding her hands, folding her hands.

Dream of room beyond room, dream of doors that don't go back.
Her violet practice, her études of yellow-tinged grape,
her butter-gold scales, her waterspot workbook, her coppery math,
her essays of strawberry spilling from mauve—she never knows
at the start of a white word in what blood blue color it ends.

Her sticky hair, aphids, every sprout a sport,
her breezes of lemon, her breath like a cinnamon-eater.

She's smiling at something in her lap, rose daughter
with a mouse in her lap, her secret,
she can't know what her secret is.

Under her overgrown acre, who knows,
rusty loppers, hollow cars,

perhaps an old stump. No one will ever look—
her maze for mice, her rabbit briar—
or climb as far as she can
past the tower where nothing
or air holds her up.

Our Mother Is Missing

Maybe she drove to the ferry, we thought,
    drove the road alongside the pasture,
threading through trees. We could imagine
    her silver car, green, silver flashes,
barred green. Something she wanted to see,
    perhaps, on the other side, in town,
a gallery, museum. Wouldn't want
    to bother us, leaving—of course we'd worry,
night, blind curves, high beams. No idea
    where she went, but maybe the ferry
to town, by pasture, through trees, and down
    the straightaway to the stop sign.
A left, to the highway, and soon she'd be passing between
    two rickety booths, Berries and Fireworks,
and on to the long run downhill
    where air sparks bright blue
so close to the water. The bridge,
    High Winds When Flashing, Caution on Grating—
but really, don't know
    where she went, we're guessing. Thought
we'd see her at dinner. Placemat, empty.
    This morning, no smell of coffee.
Should we go looking, and how,
    on the same road, craning for signs?
We might check her desk
    for a clipping or circled announcement,
her book for a calendar date.
    Don't know, we're guessing, but
she did love to stand before a painting,
    wrapped in its line, shade,
mystery. Might be there now, color glowing
    around her body. Don't know
where she went, she's missing, but she did love
    a painting to stand before,
stand wondering in,
    might be there now, its rays
all around her, her face
    alight in its light,
wondering for a long time.

Ann Tweedy

Over eighty poems of Ann Tweedy's poems have been published in journals and anthologies, including *Gertrude, Rattle, Damselfly Press*, and *Clackamas Literary Review*, and she has been nominated for a Pushcart Prize. Her chapbook *Beleaguered Oases* was published in 2010 by TcCreativePress in Los Angeles. Her manuscripts have also been selected as finalists for the Bluelight Press Annual Chapbook Competition, the Robin Becker Chapbook Contest, and the New Sins Press Poetry Book Award, among others. Originally from Massachusetts, she currently lives in Michigan, where she teaches at a law school.
www.anntweedypoetry.com

Acknowledgements

"Safety In Numbers" appears in *Clackamas Literary Review; Legal Studies Forum*

The Reader's Innocence

one day you sat reading, innocently reading–
was it you or i?–are you and i interchangeable? i confess
it was me who sat reading--as innocent as i can ever claim to be—
a poem about honeysuckle by brigit pegeen kelly,
and this poem brought the term "catherine wheel" into my vocabulary
so that now the honeysuckle has been obliterated and
crushed limbs impaled on spikes, slow bloody death
and the cheers that were said to accompany it
occupy my thoughts or flash in like those 30-second newscasts
on otherwise quiet moments. was i who chose to read this,
not knowing—of course not knowing—what it held, deprived of anything?
or is that what poetry strives for–always the unexpected?
i didn't know the poem was about honeysuckle
when i started. it had a german title that i meant to look up
but haven't, so much of letters just out of reach even
with my good education. but one of the things about agonizing
intentional deaths is that they are never out of reach, everyone
understands the fact of them and tries to imagine
what it would be like. it's only the why of them that escapes some
but perhaps not everyone. in this way they may be better subjects
than honeysuckle, which does little for me unless i imagine
plucking the flower, biting off its tender base, and sucking nectar
that the vine never meant for me to taste.

“Blue”

if i said bluebirds and stellers jays are not really blue,
that blueness is a trick their feathers are engineered
to reflect, would this mean anything
to you? as if other blueness were a state of being
separate from perception—or is it? if feathers look blue
doesn’t that make the bird blue—or blue enough—or are we
to test blue objectively to make sure it’s real, and, since birds
have been tested and fail, the whole avian kin-dom
may lay no claim to blue? this raises questions
i am not equipped to answer. for example—
my chinese friend who passes as a tribal member isn’t
indian because she passes, so maybe the birds
aren’t blue no matter how they are perceived or perceive each other.
or what about that study on race in brazil where white-
identifying people were found to have more african ancestry
than black-identifying people, so maybe feeling blue
is the operative question, but the trouble is we can ask and ask
away and the birds will never tell us. it’s also possible
that being blue in brazil means something different
than being blue in the u.s. or is blueness determined by who’s
asking the question so that i can foist my conception on birds
throughout the world? but if i couldn’t base the question
on my own conception, then i could only ever answer
a fragment of the question, which may be true after all.

and if the categorizers were to decide that blue can no longer
apply to feathers, wouldn’t bluebirds and blue jays
be forced to change the names they don’t know they have,
not to mention great blue herons who don’t look blue
anyway, except when afternoon lights up their ruffed
grey, rendering them too rich and illuminating to settle quietly
under the non-color of granite, rainydays, raccoons,
squirrels, and ash, all too flat to accommodate
the majestic heron who instead was bestowed with the honorary
but unachievable blue designation only to lose it most likely
in very short order? and what about warner brothers’ roadrunner
who’s drawn blue though real roadrunners are brown streaked in black
(save some blue skin near the eye)? could it be that the cartoon

roadrunner, that unpreyable prey, that table-turning phoenix,
is the only truly blue bird, the one real mccoy,
the post hoc archetype that all other “blue” aves
unknowingly aspire to as they fly off into equally unblue skies?

Safety In Numbers

it feels safe to be many women
at once—-confusing
but safe. alongside the lawyer, the poet,
alongside them both, the dreams
of park-ranging, running something—a laundromat
or that historic hotel in fort bidwell. always
there are escape routes, both real and imagined,
from whatever i'm doing at the moment. even my relationships
are diverse, multiple. if i tire of one me,
there's another, close at hand, to be or imagine.
true, nothing holds me very tightly
(except maybe poetry, who has my heart in its hand
no matter what i do). but for everything else
i'm like water perpetually in transition
from one form to another and then back again. and who knows
if the imagined lives proceed in a parallel universe
or if i'll ever get to live them. or how i escaped

the dangerous balance of a seemingly static life—
like that of mary, the preacher's wife from selmer tennessee,
who shot and killed the preacher
as he lay in bed, having followed his orders
for nine years according to the wifely
subordination his last sermon
propounded–like wearing during sex
the patent leather platforms
and wig that dismayed the southern jury,
like covering her bruises with make-up and lying
about how she got them,
like hiding the preacher's suffocations
of their infant daughter to make her stop.

late that tuesday night, the pressure
of being stuck got to be too much, and she
accidentally or on purpose
released bird shot into him. "i'm sorry" she said to his "why?"
before packing up and driving
their three girls to an alabama beachtown.
later she'd say working part-time at the post office
had helped her gain the confidence

to know she didn't have to
take and take it like a mouse. if only mary the preacher's wife
could have met mary the post office worker
before desperation set in, the preacher's wife
might have huddled in the arms of the worker
and forged a careful way out.

Nance Van Winckel

Nance Van Winckel's fifth collection of poems is *No Starling* (U. of Washington Press, 2007). The recipient of two NEA Poetry Fellowships and awards from the *Poetry Society of America, Poetry*, and *Prairie Schooner*, she has new poems in *Poetry Northwest, Field, The Journal*, and *Crazyhorse*. She is also the author of three collections of short fiction. She teaches in the Vermont College of Fine Arts MFA in Writing Program.

Thunderbirds Riding the Thunderhead

We woke and had
to hurry. Oaths
had been prepared for us
by the one who insists
we salute. We do,
we will. And with
nary enough time
to read the leather-bound
manual, only the odd
moment to stroke its
embossed silver letters
before the blanketed
nude selves are dressed
and carted off. Awake,
I'm aware of a duty for today:
taking the temperature
of the compost. Asleep,
I'd been sure we'd wake
as two blue flowers
in a crystal vase.

Bottled

Tight fit: you may only stand
if the bottle stands. If it tips
you do too. The stoppered air
never quite stops time.
Pour your wisp of a self into
wishes: remove his gut fat,
her gut tumor. Centurion
standby of centuries, in you
the grantings gather—all all all
to forgive the world its
lovelessness, its winds of ash
off a cold cliff. Give.
Give till it hurts. Till
the bottle breaks across a brow.
Straighten the nose. Sharpen
the tooth. Give the old gal
that piss pot of gold where
her hideous rainbow ends.

Unwilling

Keeping her night light on—
that's new. *It's okay. I lean*
over the face. Everything's fine.
Her ninetieth birthday leered
like this, then licked. Passed.

As long as the clock ticks
the teeth in the glass
won't chatter. The china bluebird
won't chirp. Prayers
for my soul trail off. . .

as the wall with my picture on it
crumbles. So long: my eyes
still watching hers
are the last to go.

Katrina Vandenberg

Katrina Vandenberg is the author of two books of poems, *The Alphabet Not Unlike the World* (2012) and *Atlas* (2004), both published by Milkweed Editions. She has received fellowships from the Fulbright, Bush, and McKnight foundations, and has been a resident at the MacDowell Colony and the Amy Clampitt House in Lenox, Massachusetts. She lives with her husband, novelist John Reimringer, in Saint Paul, Minnesota. She teaches at Hamline University.

Acknowledgments

"A Ghazal" appears in *The Southern Review*
"Cretaceous Moth Trapped in Amber (Lament in Two Voices)" appears in *Post Road*

A Ghazal

The Phoenician A is 𐤀, *aleph.* The ox points its nose forward. A
is strong enough to pull the train of letters through the poem. A.

See the yoke clutch its neck. Is the poet driving? No,
it's the man who hewed the yoke leading the ox to market, to heap A

with what he needs to get through winter. He is sending the letters
on a long drive through the early snow. What will burden A

before it can return to the barn? *A* for *alpha, most important*
—an *alpha* dog, a compelling man. A lucid star, o scarlet letter *A*

for *spontaneous abortion*, the early miscarriage's true name.
The doctor adds, "It's nothing you did," even if it does start with A,

not your fault, this bloody end to a beginning. Squeezes your hand
each time. In the beginning was the apple, round and red. A,

"Apple of my eye," your father used to say, A for the round red
embryonic sac you labored to get out. *Aardappel* starts with A—

Dutch for *potato, ground apple*, *aard* meaning *earth*, sounds like *hard*,
it's a hard world sometimes, hard-packed under oxen feet, and A

for *aardvark*, too, for *absence*, *abstain*, *absinthe*. 𐤀 sleeps
on its side in the straw. In one Nordbrandt poem I like, "A,"

"Already in the word's first letter / the word already is there /
and in the word already, the whole sentence . /. . . / as the a-

lmond tree is in each almond / and a whole almond grove in the tree. . ."
Already in the beginning was the Word, the letter A,

gold stars, *almonds*, you can have *another*, *asshole*, *and,*
alienate. "Apple of my eye," your father said, twinkling A,

that dangles from its stem, that cannot last, that gets one booted
from the garden every time. What bears fruit this time of year? "A,"

insists Nordbrandt: " . . . already in the word's first letter / the almond trees are in bloom." Saith the Lord, "I am the Alpha and the Omega."

Saith the Mother, "Already the pure child and all the unborn inside it have been forgotten with the path the ox broke through the snow: 𐤀."

M

The Berkshire hills the book that opens

again with each curve where the woods take back

what they just said ditch lilies ditch lilies

open orange eager in the Berkshires the mills

are no longer milling paper milling wool

they're milling memories of themselves

as useful they mill this skein of highway clumps

of lilies woolly thoughts the letter M its hieroglyph

a set of Mediterranean waves and the Phoenicians

who drew M first ship-makers wave-walkers

consider them first looking out then in   the mills

are milling the Housatonic river it skims

a thousand rocks is almost close enough to touch all

landscape here is intimate hemmed in a book

close to the face not *an open book* as we say

more the way a baby sees from its mother's breast

to her face and that is all an open book is

one small room its talk a little talk its form

a reinforcement of five hundred years of private

thought along with the invention of the separate

room a sudden set of separate fires the ancient

Berkshire hills their mills are milling spotted

dairy cows and woolly sheep alphabet of camels

oxen fish if my northern tribe had drawn M first

M would have been a hieroglyph for *milk* the cows

goats sheep they learned to drink from or else starve

la mer, la mère the sound of M for *mother*

in nearly every language the early sounds a baby

makes M for delicious the motor's hum delicious

drowsing off the shape of these worn-down hills the mills

mill poems walls of stone tonight they mill the stars

M for *ma*, the Japanese idea of space

and silence as a thing not absence on the radio

today they talk about the death of books

of spacious thought the book a footnote

a single clump of lilies one river thread

I think of books as milk from other animals

Cretaceous Moth Trapped in Amber

(Lament in Two Voices)

What a shame I have nothing to give you but midnight, my story
Little moth caught forever in the last moment of before,

of five French soldiers with identically shaved heads,
when the dusk was thick with incense and crickets

the one who spit in my hair, the one who slapped me,
and great northern evergreens wept puddles of resin

the one who kissed my mouth as the others watched.
on the forest floor. What were you stammering toward

Their green nylon jackets, their laced boots, their laughter,
the night you got stuck, a moon lost in thought

the glass wall of the lit phone booth they pushed me against.
as it cast its glistening net over tree frogs, over the mites

I got away. But when I reached my unlit street
punctuating the laddered webs of orb weavers,

and they were still following me, I had to choose:
over the orb weavers about to be lodged in resin

break for the host family's door? Or light back
themselves? This is the story now under glass,

to the phone booth, to the main drag, where
honeyed and see-through: a palm of red-gold

yellow headlights kept slipping by? I wanted
beads traded for swords and furs in the Viking town

home. I chose the glass box, though I feared it a trap.
of Dublin. And in millions of years

I moved toward the lights.
the moon has not changed; it is still perched

Today I know that saved my life.
in its starry web, dropping its sticky strands.

But you know what I am saying, moth.
The world has not changed; there is still a great deal

It could have just as easily been different.
of getting caught in it, you must choose.

Photograph of My Parents' First Christmas

Kind of like the Pietà but set in working-class Detroit:
            my mother perches on my father's lap, her shift

celery-green, not unlike something Gidget might have worn.

My father's biceps bulge; he stares the camera down.
            She tilts her head toward the puppy stretched

across their laps. The room? Mostly empty. Console

television's gray-faced. A stiff new easy chair
            that will grow more easy through my childhood,

a tree decked out in silver, blue. You have to look

hard to see the tension in their arms
            as they push down the half-trained puppy

to hold it still. When they shamed it for failing

to be good, I bet it cringed, then shook
            an old balled-up sock of my father's in its teeth.

I bet they laughed; they wanted things to work.

Sarah Vap

Sarah Vap is the author of three books of poetry, *Dummy Fire* (which received the 2006 Saturnalia Poetry Prize), *American Spikenard* (which received the 2006 Iowa Poetry Prize) and, most recently, *Faulkner's Rosary* (Saturnalia Books, 2010).

Acknowledgments

"Hold," "Take us the foxes," "Night," and "Breathing loaf of wild animal" appear in *American Poetry Review*

Take us the foxes

I didn't know, when I'd never made love,
the sounds that I would make then—

like that, I didn't know

the sound of my fear: cry

like the faraway animal. Deep
animal moan,

from somewhere else and a quiet
stay, stay

chanted where the gold edge

and the warm night met. When I was a child

I knew the details
of each foal's birth—the chestnut, catching

her first breath in her mother's shit-covered tail.

Her hooves, still soft and curled underneath
as a human ear,

pawed the dead udder. When the sun
rose on her I thought:

could any light be pale

lapping onto this world. Could any surface

glossed—a bed of snow, the bed of the river—
fall flat against the world

that holds us in?

Hold

A baby can't love himself, I think. Plum,
magenta

reversals of light—a cloth ball

to roll to the baby. His is the more decent
dark radiance—he is still a baby

picking through a pile of yarn. My son might watch
the beautiful things disappear. Yet,

where my remembrance joins his reminiscence—

as scraps of paper on the floor, or a few
purple tiles. Who, on the advice of her soul alone,

could be the counterweight

of his plain light. But the final color
is different, as something permanent is.

As an heir to memory is, or as a love
that will hurt us.

Breathing loaf of wild animal

Selah, I said to you once, paint my eyes
black at their edges. Blue powder that glows

in the grease. Did I say it when I held our son up
above my head, laughing so hard my milk

fell out of his mouth to the edge of my eye.
But who would hear of milk

or of this joy,

we are tired of women and children.

Tired of a woman's painted eye
which has not stopped us,

and God has not stopped us. The possibility
is different

where free and where wild have lived
in the adoring mind. The blackening woods at evening

are beside me, pulling rabbits. Pulling rabbits.

Night

The three of us watch, holding hands,
a children's roller coaster in the shape of a dragon, as if someone

loved could disappear without residue. Without a stain

of love somewhere on earth. Christ salted his fish.
Tore the column of bones

out along its back. Small and true things
of abundance—perhaps I once believed

you were knowable. You tell our son the story
of the talking babydoll, cooked into a loaf of bread that hollers

Mama, Mama

from the oven. The babydoll the dragon and Jesus,

you say, are each the other's world entire. It's better, simply, to say
that now we know each other.

To say that now

I can whisper something to you,
and it didn't hurt.   Our evening

of air and silver, and oh God you
have chosen to live this life with me. And you

will do this to me, then tell me the story of our sons

racing a line of cartwheels to the apple tree and back
to crawl

down a single lock of my hair
each night. Touch my face, and then we all sleep.

Kary Wayson

Kary Wayson's poems have appeared in *Crazyhorse, Poetry Northwest, Alaska Quarterly Review, The Nation, The Journal, Field, Filter, The Best American Poetry 2007*, and the *2010 Pushcart Prize* anthology. Kary was a 2003 Discovery/The Nation award winner, and her chapbook, *Dog & Me*, was published in 2004 by LitRag Press. Her first full collection, *American Husband*, won the Ohio State University Press/*The Journal* Award in 2009. Kary lives and works in Seattle.

Acknowledgments

"Flu Song in Spanish" appears in *Alaska Quarterly Review*, reprinted in *Best American Poetry 2007*
"More of the Same" appears in *Mass. Ave.*, reprinted in (and forthcoming from) *Poetry International*
"Double Down" appears in *The Journal*
"If English" appears in *LitRag*

All of the poems appear in *American Husband* (Ohio State University Press, 2009)

Flu Song In Spanish

God of the bees, god of gold keys, god of all in-
famous noses, I folded our total
in two today-I drove alone
and I walked away (as if each mile up your hill
were a letter in a word I'm inventing).
So I stuck my head in a hole and stood.
So far so. So far
good. Now I wear that hole like a hood
in a house
of inscrutable signals.

God of the guess, god of the gap
mind if I make you a martyr?
If the sky says anything, it's everything! at once!
(Nor did you answer my question.)
So I stick my head in a hole and stand. So far
so far. So far, grand. Sand in my pants and ants
in the box, I wish there were bells
for when I should stop.
Show me the bell for when I should stop!
(Not that I'd know when to ring it.)

Grant me the grace and I'll fix it. Shit.
My father (that bitch!) he hides
at the head
of his third wife's table.
The man says one thing then
nothing. For months.
(Though I've always been welcome to dinner.)
So I stook my head in a hole instead.
So far: slow car: a sofa bed. A brick in the back
where he buries the dead. His task is her
two daughters.

God of the aster, God of disaster, God of
charisma and risk: if a word and a wing
are the same stringy thing
then what in the world can I say?
The sign means too much: you translate

my hunch (there's no chance in hell today).
So I stick my head in a hole and drown. So far
lost, so far I found a bone-cutter's house
in a blood-lit town: I swear I'll tear your eyes away.

Double Down

I try to make a poem in order to be smart
about the way one do walked
when he wanted to run around.

Look at my dead dog now!

Demonstrated in the slant flight of a seaplane in the sky
where someone is devoting himself
to a direction I recognize.

Smudge of a dog, up and to the west, I try.

Looking to the left while I'm walking
to the right, I move
en masse, as if stuck on a raft
with my enemies.
It gets so awkward inside of me. Look:
now I'm out back, berating the garden.

My umbrella isn't in case but the cause of the worst
rain coming down.

My soul is shaped like a shovel buried in the ground.

If English

If geography is the highway I take to your house,
then geology is the house, the cliff it sits on,
the cross hairs the frames cast on the yellow walls.
Geometry is the windows into the living room
and entomology is the key under the brick by the back door.
Biology, then, is the bathroom,
and the shower with you singing inside it
a lecture on erosion in a conservation class.
Chemistry is the kitchen, the feta cheese on the counter,
and how many leaves is calculus
collected in the corner by the pot of wilted daffodils.
The brother's abandoned bedroom is history: his globe,
his football helmet, his ratty blue bathrobe.
And if the front porch is philosophy
with eye-screws in the rafters where a swing should be,
then theology is the front door ajar.
In English I'd say English
is the telephone and the telephone book
and the table with one vase and the cut rose.
Belief would be the unmade bed
and any discussion of God, your body
still sleeping beside your clothes.

More Of The Same

But even with my mouth on your thigh
I want my mouth on your thigh.
At the center bite of bread I want the whole loaf
toasted, and an orange. On a sunny day
I want more sun, more skin for the weather.
I'm in Seattle wishing for Seattle,
for this walk along the water, for her hand while I hold it:
I want to tie my wrist to a red balloon.
I'm counting my tips.
I'm counting the tips I could have made.
I want the television on, the television off.
In the ocean, I want to float an inch above it
and when my father finally held me
like a stripe of seaweed over his wet arm,
I was kicking to get away, wishing he'd hold me
like he held me while I was kicking away. Listen to me.
I want to leave when I'm walking out the door.

Katharine Whitcomb

Katharine Whitcomb is the author of a collection of poems, *Saints of South Dakota & Other Poems*, which was chosen by Lucia Perillo as the winner of the 2000 Bluestem Award and published by Bluestem Press, and two poetry chapbooks. *Hosannas* (Parallel Press, 1999) and *Lamp of Letters* (Floating Bridge Press, 2009), winner of the 2009 Floating Bridge Chapbook Award. Her poetry awards include a Stegner Fellowship at Stanford University. She lives in Ellensburg, Washington.

Poem Without Ferocity

Deep breath before drinking morning coffee.
Outside in the wind, leaves blaze greening sap, lit
fuses. April slides to May more luscious
each day. My lover drives away early
as I sometimes do across town, to the squawking
of crows. We leave each other happy, intent on the day.
I could live inside of April the way the air reverberates
now—frogs singing *wake up,* and I'm already awake.

Lines for Mid-Winter

Time was we threw an annual solstice party to burn our burdens
—sent flaming tongue depressor boats downriver with a cargo of curling photos
of old boyfriends and bad habits scrawled on scraps.

We waved goodbye from the shore and made lists of good wishes.

This year I cannot do it. Instead, I stomp a big circle through the snow
a thousand footprints around the house and do not raise my face once,
though the birds overhead are hungry and I hear them.

For me, no more trying on shirts for a turn before the mirror;
no dreaming like a princess under my quilts.

I walk a big circle without faith in my convictions.
I am not young or uncomplicated or down-to-earth.

The future is candle-flame painted by Gerhard Richter.
The future is a lost dog by the road.

Inside my house a lamp is lit.
Through the window, the walnut bookcase
looks for a moment broad-shouldered and tall, like someone else.

Wendy Wisner

Wendy Wisner is the author of a book of poems, *Epicenter* (WordTech, 2004), and a chapbook, *Another Place of Rocking* (Pudding House Press, 2010). Her poems have appeared in numerous journals and anthologies, including *The Spoon River Review, The Bellevue Literary Review, Rhino, Natural Bridge, 5AM*, and *Verse Daily*. Wendy taught writing and literature at Hunter College for four years. Since the birth of her son in 2007, she has pursued her long-time interest in women's health and babies: she volunteers as a breastfeeding counselor, and is pursuing her Lactation Consultant (IBCLC) certification.
www.wendywisner.com

Acknowledgments

"Eve" appears in *Cutthroat*

Eve

Wandering naked after love,
I cover myself with the wet leaf
of my open hand.

The uncovered
window, fumes from our
neighbor's garden snaking through.

We want a child. Is that too much
to ask? We know
the world's a dark place.

Yesterday we saw a family
of starlings lumbering up the fire escape.

What ever happened
to flying? God,
have you taken it
away from us completely?

Give it back. Let a child
flutter inside me.

Penelope and Lucy

Watering our plants,
gazing at last night's thin layer

of snow, I hear you shuffling behind me
like a kid still in his PJ's.

You peer over my shoulder to watch
how I douse each plant with too much

water, how I let the water spill
over the edge of the windowsill.

Months ago, we'd named the plants:
Penelope and Lucy, our two green girls.

We'd imagined a human girl
ticking inside me, taking root.

Now we're cheek to cheek, breathing in
the pale February morning.

Before I lost the baby, I dreamt
I held her to my face,

her fat soft cheek wet against me.

Quickening

After lunch, I lean back on the couch
and you tap me from deep inside.
I'm not ready for this, I say,
and you tap me again.
It's August, heat fogging up the window.
It doesn't matter what I want.
Thunder tonight, I think,
but it doesn't matter what I think.
You hide inside me
and all around us summer
like the summer my mother was born—
even she doesn't matter anymore.

Nine Months

October. Gray leaves, dark berries. The baby
crawling out of my arms. Fog. Humid rain.
He's been out as long as he was in.

Shadows on the hardwood floor, he and I
rocking in the dark. A tenderness between us.
Beauty: his fist in the nape of my neck.

Hazy window. Books, scarves, toys
strewn on the floor. My father in the doorway.
Is he leaving? Is he coming home?

Nine months. The body remembers:
A rustling beneath the skin. Red leaves
igniting, branches bursting buds, his body

rising inside me.

Rachel Zucker

Rachel Zucker is the author of seven books, most recently *Museum of Accidents* and (with Arielle Greenberg) *Home/Birth: a poemic*. She lives in New York City with her husband and their three sons. She teaches poetry at NYU and is a certified birth doula. www.rachelzucker.net

Acknowledgments

"I Do Not Like Your Job" and "Fridays" appear in *Poor Claudia*
"One You Pass This Point You Must Continue to Exit" appears in *Lowball*

I Do Not Like Your Job

there's no chance you'll have sex with me at 3:15 pm which is one minute from now because you are at the place called work and it takes 20-65 minutes to get home from there depending on whether you drive or ride the subway and anyway you can't leave early because it's necessary to impress upon the right people you'd like to stay at this place called job even after your contract expires and you're so new you don't even know who to impress and I suspect no one in the department would appreciate my desire to copulate at 3:15 pm and the 20-65 minute preparations it would require of you and this sacrifice isn't even the worst part for either of us truth is you didn't have a job for 10 years and we never made love in the afternoon you don't like to I do but it takes two I'm lying here reading poetry which makes me horny I won't say whose it's not *him* though he *is* a hunk just the act of reading anything in the last moments of a toddler's nap such sweet silence this is my "work" I suppose but utterly different from yours I'm embarrassed to admit I just delighted myself with two squares of dark chocolate this is literally one of the ten "days of awe" I'd like to make the most of it to be honest it's not just reading I think it's how this poet writes about loving his wife I find titillating nothing quite so attractive as a man hot for his wife except maybe an innocent-looking boyman transformed by a guitar and a stage that's someone's job but 'hot for his wife' isn't a profession I don't think not yours anyway and that's why I hate your job

Fridays

Good shoppers trampled a man
to death. Does laziness save lives?
I meant my laziness by which I mean
the many ways I keep my kids
alive and the few words I put aside
for later. Be kind, mothers say,
to yourself and others. This is
an old topic and the only one.
Today I want to trample my own
heart. Here they come: sudden
onset of the end of loneliness.

Once You Pass This Point You Must Continue to Exit

in memory of Peggy Sradnick

What they say   People who are still alive   Say   And I'm   Through space&time
Not going to   Anyone

As we all will she   Why do the details make us feel   safe

The plane opens its body to me   Am alive

Still   Morning   On the plane in the coffeeshop in bed in traffic   Among
The living   "How"   Doesn't protect   Anyone

I'm leaking   Then cracking open   Here, here, here   The alive
Splinter   In me

Our neighborhood   Alive everywhere   This makes   Nothing
Meaningful

How are you?   Alive
How are you?   Not here
Am

Where else would   I   Funeral   This   To be this this tired one must be must be

Let it in   She is

What do I even like to eat?   What is?   Someone?   Too

How are you?   How?   Did did did   ?

Nothing   Traveled here   To do

What they say about   Talk about   As a subject   She's
dead

Alive people   Airport taxi plane   Alive people   They say she   Then she
When How
She

I say, the way she said my name my whole name when I called

These Details We Nothing

the young men crying are 23 I can't when they say she changed my life no one this is what makes life meaning this unbearable without which let it in I will not stop on the plane taxi sidewalk everyone no one over and over and over this happens if you are lucky enough to be loved so much as to cause this kind of suffering.

I'd Like a Little Flashlight

and I'd like to get naked and into bed and be hot. Radiating heat from the inside
these sweaters and fleecies do nothing to keep out the out or keep my vitals in—
some drafty body I've got leaking in and out in all directions I'd like to get naked
into bed but hot on this early winter afternoon already dusky grim and not think of
all the ways I've gone about the world and shown myself a fool, shame poking holes
in my thinned carapace practically lacy and woefully feminine I'd like to get naked
into bed and feel if not hot then weightless as I once was in the sensory deprivation
tank in Madison, Wisconsin circa 1992 I paid money for that perfectly body-
temperatured silent pitch dark tank to do what—play dead and not die? That was
before email before children before I knew anything more than the deaths of a few
loved ones which were poisoned nuts of swallowed grief but nothing of life, of life
giving, which cuts open the self bursting, busted, unsolvable always I'd like to get
naked into the bed of my life but hot, *hot* my little flicker self inside trumped up
somehow blind and deaf to all the dampening misery of my friends' woe oh ohs and
I'd like a little flashlight to write poems with this lousy day not this poem I'm
writing under the mostly flat blaze of bulb but a poem written with the light itself a
tiny fleeting love poem to life—hot hot hot—a poem that would say *oh look here a
bright spot of life, oh look another!*

Editors' Bios

Kelli Russell Agodon is the author of *Letters from the Emily Dickinson Room* (White Pine Press, 2010), Winner of the Foreword Magazine Book of the Year Prize in Poetry and Washington State Book Award Finalist. She is also the author of *Small Knots* (2004) and *Geography,* winner of the 2003 Floating Bridge Press Chapbook Award. She is the co-editor of Seattle's literary journal, *Crab Creek Review* and the co-founder of Two Sylvias Press. She enjoys mountain biking, dessert, and reading eBooks on her iPad.

Kelli blogs at Book of Kells: www.ofkells.blogspot.com And connect with her on Facebook at: www.facebook.com/agodon or her website: www.agodon.com

~

Annette Spaulding-Convy's full length collection, *In Broken Latin*, will be published by the University of Arkansas Press (Fall 2012) as a finalist for the Miller Williams Poetry Prize. Her chapbook, *In The Convent We Become Clouds*, won the 2006 Floating Bridge Press Chapbook Contest and was nominated for a Pushcart Prize. Her poems have appeared in *Prairie Schooner, North American Review, Crab Orchard Review* and in the *International Feminist Journal of Politics*, among others. She is co-editor of the literary journal, *Crab Creek Review*, and is co-founder of Two Sylvias Press. She enjoys reading eBooks on her Nook.

CPSIA information can be obtained
at www.ICGtesting.com
Printed in the USA
FSOW02n2054220916
25300FS